Yum Yum Cha

LET'S EAT DIM SUM in Hawai'i

Yum Yum Cha

LET'S EAT DIM SUM in Hawai'i

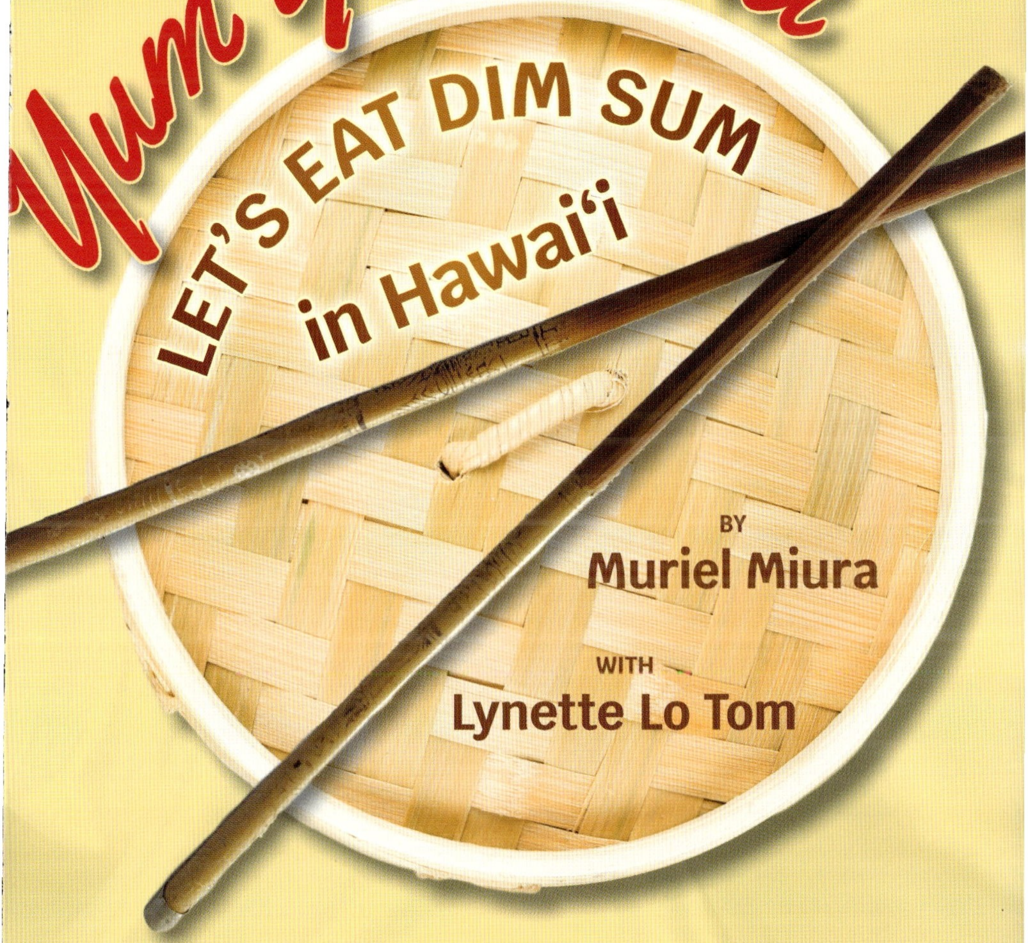

BY
Muriel Miura

WITH
Lynette Lo Tom

Mutual Publishing

Library of Congress Control Number 2021949700

ISBN: 978-1-949307-29-0

First Printing, November 2021
Second Printing, January 2023

Mutual Publishing, LLC
1215 Center Street, Suite 210
Honolulu, Hawai'i 96816
Ph: 808-732-1709 / Fax: 808-734-4094
email: info@mutualpublishing.com
www.mutualpublishing.com

Printed in South Korea

Food illustrations by Paul Konishi
Photos by Lynette Lo Tom: pg. iii (chopsticks), xvii-xviii, xxv, xxviii, 2-3, 5-6, 11-14, 16-18, 21, 25-26, 28, 33, 35, 40-41, 43-45, 48, 52, 56, 59, 64, 66-67, 69-71, 74, 77-78, 84 (peanuts), 87 (slab sugar)-88, 90-92, 95-96, 98-102, 106, 114, 118-120, 125-126, 130, 132, 134, 137-138, 140, 143, 152, 156, 166, 179 (both), 180
Photo by *Honolulu Star-Advertiser*: pg. 194
Photos by Kaz Tanabe: pg. xii, 27, 76, 84 (spoon with peppercorns), 123, 128, 150, 177 (bitter melon), 178 (both)
Photos by Darien Moriguchi: pg. 8, 168
Photos by Taren Taguchi: pg. 36, 38
Photo by Malcom Mekaru and Olivier Koning: pg. 196
Photo by Christie Wilson: pg. 7
Photos from www.freepik.com: pg. i, ii, iii (steamer basket), vi-vii (backgrounds), 87 (sesame seeds), 97, 107
Photos from www.dreamstime.com: pg. xxiv, 32, 50, 93, 104, 110, 127, 153, 163, 177 (gai lan)

To Alissa and Stephen Ling

Written with love,
Muriel

To Chloe Kokoro Kanda and Theo David Lin

With much love and aloha,
Lynette

Chinese food
is for the pleasure
of the stomach,

French food
is for the pleasure
of the nose,

Japanese food
is for the pleasure
of the eyes.

—*old saying*

CONTENTS

Dumplings

Bao (Buns), Rolls, and Bread

Other Dim Sum

Sweets

OTHER DISHES

Vegetables

Rice & Noodles

Sauces

Muriel Miura and Betty Shimabukuro co-authored the books What Hawai'i Likes to Eat *and* Hawai'i's Holiday Cookbook *and co-edited the "Hawai'i Cooks" series.*

FOREWORD
BY BETTY SHIMABUKURO

Muriel Miura was my cookbook-writing partner for more than a decade, and through all those years, in just about every conversation, she'd mention the dim sum cookbook she hoped to complete one day. It seemed to be a holy grail for her—a departure, as it was, from her usual collection of Japanese, island-style, or straightforward family recipes. But in a way, I see this Chinese collection as a deeper reflection of Muriel's cooking philosophy.

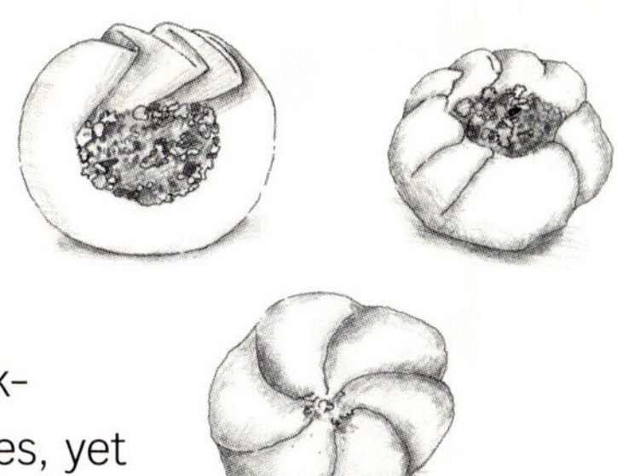

Muriel believed in no-nonsense cooking and professed to hate "fussy" recipes, yet dim sum is meticulous work, not quick and easy. Dim sum takes clever fingers and the patience to fold and crimp, over and over, to make a variety of items into a cohesive, attractive meal. But while it's true that Muriel's cookbooks generally lean toward simple dishes, a similar focus on creating beauty on a plate is reflected in many of her more complex recipes.

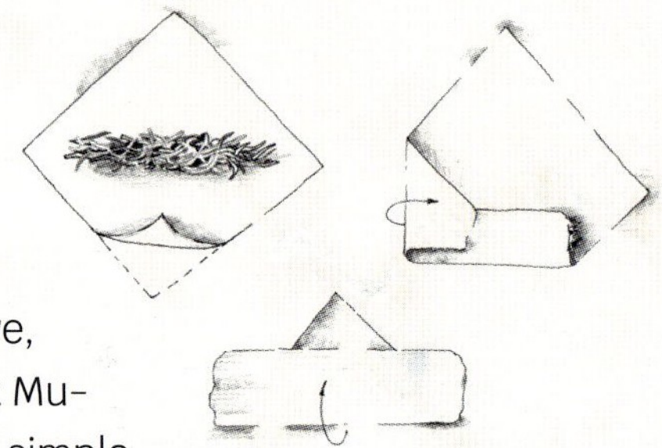

Above all, Muriel saw preparing food for others as an expression of caring. To take the time to craft a pleasing selection of small bites—be they sushi or dim sum—is to express devotion, both to those at the table and to the respective culinary art.

Muriel collected these recipes and nuggets of dim sum lore over many years, but sadly, when she died in 2020 the book remained unfinished. Instead, Lynette Lo Tom has completed Muriel's work and I can't think of anyone better for the task. Lynette has few rivals in Hawai'i when it comes to knowledge of Chinese cuisine and reverence for its traditions. Although it must have taken considerable effort to piece together another writer's thoughts through only her recipes and notes, this book reads as though Lynette worked on it side by side with Muriel.

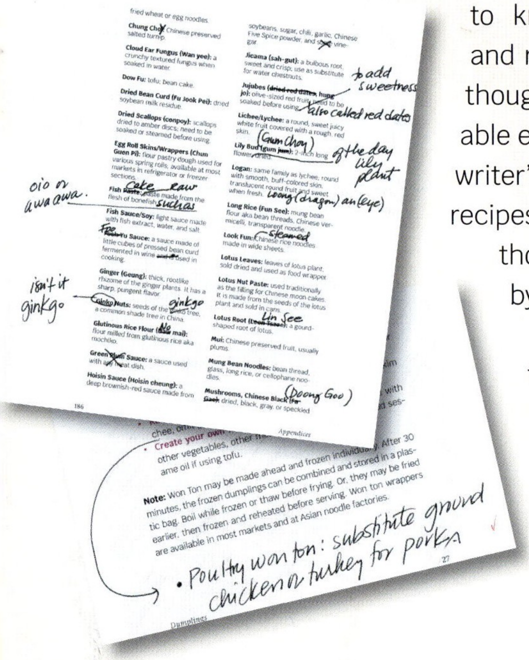

They are two very different food writers, but in this collection their approaches merge in a respect for a culinary tradition meant to "touch the heart."

MAHALO
FROM MURIEL

I would like to express my deepest gratitude to my family and friends who, for years, patiently assisted me in compiling, testing, tasting, and editing the dim sum recipes featured in this book.

I also greatly appreciate the kindness, cooperation, and courtesy of the owners, managers, and staff of my favorite dim sum restaurants in Honolulu, New York, San Francisco, and Maryland. I would be remiss if special thanks isn't extended to the Mandalay Chinese Restaurant of Honolulu and its owner/manager, Linda Chan, for her assistance regarding the history of dim sum.

Thanks to Paul Konishi, the talented illustrator of this book whose unlimited talents go beyond illustrations.

MAHALO
FROM LYNETTE

As an editor for my first cookbook, *A Chinese Kitchen*, Muriel Miura was a great teacher in showing me how recipes could be more clearly understood by a beginning cook. She was a role model with her gentle way of questioning. It is an honor to finish the cookbook she told me about many years ago; a tribute to her grandchildren.

I would like to thank the "village" of friends who helped me with this cookbook: Taren Taguchi and Debbie Lau Okamura, who encouraged me to write a cookbook years ago. My mother, Lorna Lee Lo, and grandparents, Louise Ho Lo, John Sau Lee, and Florence Wong Lee, who were great cooks and sources of inspiration.

Yen Chun has so much knowledge about Chinese culture and generously helped with romanization and insights. Charlene Lo Chan and Wesley Chan, who gave me input about dim sum in San Francisco. June Kam Tong of Popo's Kitchen, Liana Benn of Royal Kitchen, Kristie Ou and Zhi Qiang Ou of Taipan Dim Sum Restaurant, Michelle Cheung, Linda Bessara, Elton Lee, Alex Hsieh, Joanne Pating, and others who shared recipes and techniques. Deborah Yu Cooney, Mary Rose Shen, and Eimi Zecha who shared stories about Hong Kong and Shanghai dim sum.

Andrew Mau of the Char Hung Sut Mau family who shared stories and memories.

Ongoing supporters Aileen Fuke, Ann Harakawa, Darien Moriguchi, Anne Scherf, Christie Wilson, and Cassandra Pan. Chefs Ed Kenney, Dave Caldiero, Alika Chung, and Regino Ojano, III.

Friends who donated their time as proofreaders: Lani Abrigana, Charlene Lo Chan, Becky Choy, Kathy Inkinen, Julie Krucky, Robyn Kuraoka, Bonni Sue Lee, Laurie Jean Lee, Marlene Nakamoto, Deborah Lau Okamura, Melanie Okazaki, Nalani Parry, Floyd Takeuchi, Cathy Tanaka, Joyce Timpson, Elisa Yadao, and Ann Yoshida. Please excuse me if I have forgotten anyone.

And the most dedicated supporter of all, my husband Neal Kanda, who is chief proofreader, critic, and patient food taster.

Thank you all so much for your love and support of my art.

A NOTE ON SPELLING

Although Chinese characters are recognized by all throughout the Chinese diaspora, romanization, or the method of translating the characters into English words, varies by region. In China, almost every region spoke a different dialect. More than 75 to 80 percent of the Chinese plantation workers in Hawai'i arrived from a small subregion of Canton (now called Guangzhou); the predominant pronunciation of words is that area's Zhong Shan-style. Dim sum originated in the Canton region and for many years, Hong Kong was considered the world's center for the best dim sum, so many names for dishes are the Hong Kong style.

However, various ethnic groups have influenced what we say in Hawai'i. For example, Char Siu Bao, a soft steamed bun with a filling of sweet, marinated barbecued pork, is called manapua in Hawai'i. We refer to the baked version and the steamed version by the same name. It comes from the native Hawaiian language where mea ono means pastry or cake and pua'a means pig or pork.

Another popular dim sum is called Gok Jai in Hawai'i and Fan Gwo ouside Hawai'i, a tender, yet chewy translucent covering with a mixed filling of chopped pork and bamboo shoots. It also could be spelled Kok Chai. Here in Hawai'i, it is also called Half Moon or Pepeiao in the Hawaiian language for its shape like an ear. However, pepeiao is also the local nickname for the fungus growing on trees (called elephant ears or mok ngee).

The basic pronunciation could be close or a slight variation. What we call Jin Dui, the delicious dessert with a chewy fried glutinous rice dough outside and sweet filling inside, could be also spelled Chien Doi.

In a few cases, we have used the Mandarin Chinese (now called Pu Tong Hwa in China) for northern dishes. If you speak to someone from China or from Taiwan, the words will differ.

We have attempted to give you the most common spelling for these delicious morsels. Please excuse us if we did not use your favorite spellings.

INTRODUCTION

A favorite culinary outing is a dim sum brunch or lunch. It offers a wide variety of savory treats such as dumplings, filled buns, spring rolls, and other bite-sized treats to sample and enjoy. The petite portions stimulate one's appetite and the variety of dim sum seems endless.

Dim sum, a Cantonese phrase which means "touch the heart," is linked to the Chinese tradition of "yum cha," or drinking tea, and is also the term used to describe the dining experience. Yum cha is an ancient Chinese teahouse tradition which accommodated weary travelers over the centuries.

One could argue that eating the foods at yum cha is to sample the best of Chinese food or at least southern Chinese cuisine. The servings are small, usually three items or fewer, placed on a small plate, so you can take one bite and still have the appetite to savor many more dishes.

Served with steaming pots of fragrant Chinese tea, dim sum cuisine includes a wide variety of choices such as combinations of seafood, vegetables, meat, as well as desserts and fruit. Today, dim sum is a popular luncheon or weekend morning treat for many throughout the world.

Dim sum started in southern China, but it's now served throughout China with the addition of many northern Chinese dishes. Northern breads such as the fluffy, tender, unfilled bun called Mantou or the

popular green onion chewy pancakes (Chun Yau Bang) are sometimes flavored with crushed Sichuan peppercorns.

To bring the pleasures of dim sum home, here are recipes from travels, friends, and family over the years. Some are traditional, like Siu Mai (pork hash), where others have been revised to make them more appealing to the modern palate. The selection of dim sum in this cookbook reflects the uniqueness of Hawai'i with such favorites as Baked and Steamed Barbecue Pork Buns—known as Char Siu Bao or Manapua—and the ever popular Gok Jai—which we refer to as the half moon or pepeiao (the Hawaiian word for ear) due to its shape.

Many of the dishes would make sumptuous appetizers. Serve them as a delicious grazing menu—they can be easily managed for any sized group. Just mix and match dishes to provide a range of flavors, textures, and temperatures using a variety of interesting containers such as bamboo or metal steamers and heat-resistant dishes of various shapes and sizes. For presentation, line the serving platter with ti leaves, banana leaves, or shredded romaine. Serve the sauces separately. Enjoy.

ORDERING DIM SUM

Now, because of pandemic concerns, the wonderful hustle and bustle of servers rolling dim sum carts is not always offered. Those carts, filled with an assortment of delicacies and moving between tables and booths, had such a wide variety of offerings. The lighter, steamed dishes come first and are followed by more adventurous items such as braised chicken feet, then deep-fried dishes and ending with a tasty dessert. However, in Hawai'i, this protocol is rarely followed and eager diners order their favorite foods as fast as they can.

Where the cart system has been discontinued, a dim sum menu is placed on the table and a pencil is used to select items and the food is served at the table in steamer baskets.

Pricing of dishes may vary, but traditionally the dishes are classified as "small," "medium," "large," or "special order" (a menu item not typically considered a dim sum item such as an order of chow fun). The dishes ordered may be recorded on a bill at the table or servers may use distinct stamps on a card on the table to track sales statistics for each server. Another method of pricing the food consumed uses colored dishes left on the diner's table whereby a price is designated for each colored dish.

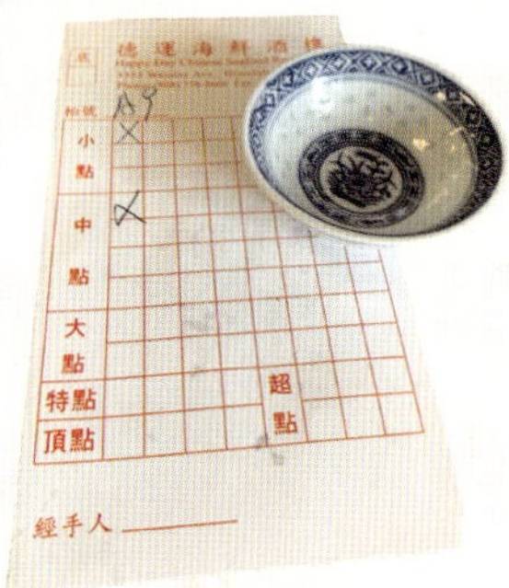

The challenge in recreating the dim sum experience at home is to offer an array of food like one finds at dim sum tea houses or restaurants. Each of those dishes requires as much, or more, work to prepare as a regular, full-course dinner.

To enjoy dim sum at home, keep it simple. Pick and choose a few of the recipes that you enjoy preparing and serving, make enough for a group, and enjoy a special eating experience. If you are just beginning in this cooking arena, start with a simple dumpling and make two sauces. For example, start by making boiled Wonton Pork Dumplings (page 26) and serve them with a Spicy Soy Dipping Sauce (page 172) and a Ginger Dipping Sauce (page 176).

DIM SUM EQUIPMENT & SUPPLIES

You'll find the following items helpful, but not essential in making dim sum.

Cheesecloth—line steamers with several layers of dampened cheesecloth when steaming breads. The cheesecloth absorbs moisture and prevents the breads from becoming soggy. You can also use a clean dish towel.

Chinese cleaver—a heavy knife with a broad, rectangular-shaped blade. A very versatile utensil, it is used to cut, slice, chop, shred, and mince all types of meats and vegetables.

Chinese curved spatula—a slightly curved spatula which is used for cooking everything in the wok.

Chopsticks—not only do they serve as eating utensils, but they are used in the kitchen for stirring, mixing, whipping, and sorting. They are available in a variety of shapes and sizes and are made from various materials such as bamboo, coral, gold, silver, wood, and plastic. There are long chopsticks (about 20 inches) and short ones (5 inches), round and angled ones. Long wooden or bamboo chopsticks are recommended for cooking.

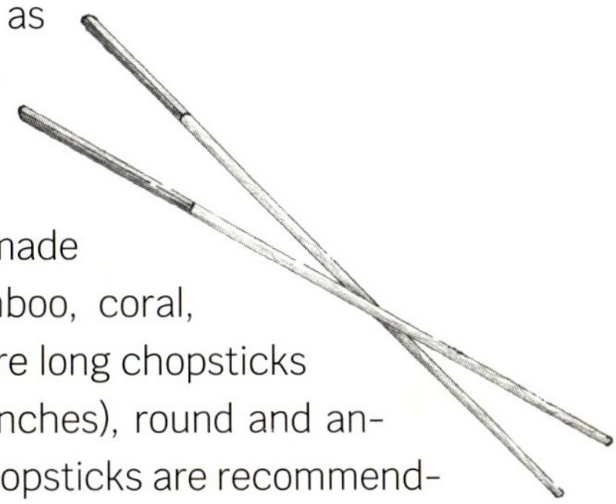

Heat-proof dishes—8- to 9-inch round or square glass or stainless cake, pie pans or porcelain plates. These can be the same pans you use for baking.

Ladle—a metal ladle used for serving soups and numerous dishes.

Parchment paper—cut into squares and use under steamed items to keep them from sticking to the pan. Do not use waxed paper.

Pastry brush—the use of a soft pastry brush with bristles or silicone makes it easier to brush the tops of the various dim sum evenly with egg wash.

Rolling pins—a standard rolling pin is best for rolling out dumpling or pastry dough and a miniature (8 inches long and about 1 inch in diameter) is best for small rounds of dough. A straight-sided bottle or a finely sanded dowel greased lightly with vegetable oil also works.

Skillets—a non-stick skillet is preferred to prevent batter or dough from sticking and requires less oil for cooking. A cast-iron skillet approaches the high heat needed from a wok.

Steamers—many steamed dishes are cooked over boiling water and the plate of food is kept elevated above the water level like in a wok with a tight-fitting lid or a large pot. Other popular steamers are the multi-tiered metal or bamboo steamers.

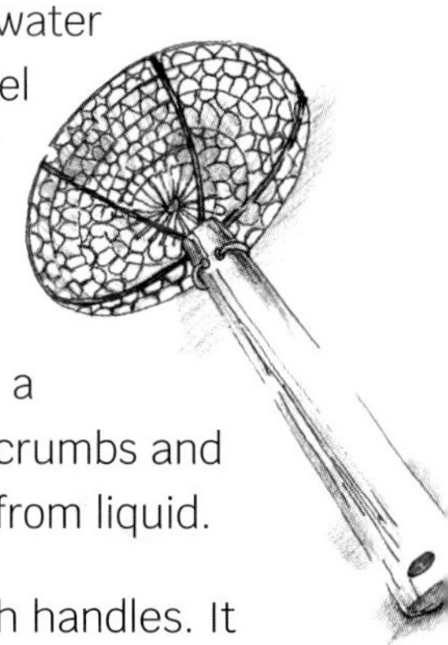

Wire skimmer—also called a spider; a metal utensil with a fine to medium wire mesh which may be used to remove crumbs and things from liquids, as well as to strain or remove noodles from liquid.

Wok—a Chinese cooking pan shaped like a salad bowl with handles. It is usually made of iron, aluminum, or copper and is used for everything from stir-frying, braising, stewing, steaming, or deep-frying. If you do not have a wok, substitute a cast-iron skillet as it can come close to achieving the high temperatures needed.

Wok cover—a metal, high domed lid with a handle that is useful while cooking.

Wok ring or **Wok holder**—a metal ring perforated with holes to hold the round-bottomed wok steady while cooking on a range.

TIME FOR TEA

According to legend, tea was discovered many centuries ago when a Chinese scholar was boiling water and a few leaves fell into his pot. The refreshing taste of his new creation was greatly appreciated by all who experienced its calming and healing powers. Although the history of tea is steeped in religion and medicine, one doesn't have to be a guru to appreciate and enjoy a cup of this soothing brew. The popularity of tea has exploded around the world and is a staple in China.

Most experts on tea agree that tea drinking originated in China and historical writings reveal that the tea plant was cultivated there as early as the fourth century B.C.

All teas are grown in a humid climate and come from the dried leaves of the *Camellia sinensis* plant. The way the leaves are processed determines a tea's style. During harvesting, the top two leaves and buds of the plant are plucked, then dried, oxidized, and heated to stop oxidation. There are more than 250 kinds of Chinese teas.

CHOOSE YOUR TEA

In general, the main types of Chinese tea are black, green, and oolong, which make up about ninety-four percent of all tea consumed in the world. Black tea is oxidized the longest, therefore it has the strongest flavor. Green tea is much milder because it is dried for just a few hours and isn't oxidized or heated. Oolong tea lies somewhere between black and green tea in terms of oxidation and flavor.

UNFERMENTED—known as green tea with a natural bouquet and light color. It is made by drying fresh leaves to prevent them from fermenting. The tea is usually rolled and twisted to uncurl while steeping in hot water.

- **Dragon Well** or **Loong Ching (Long Jing),** a mellow green tea that is most famous and is prized for its bright color and cooling effect.
- **Gunpowder,** also known as the pearl tea or zhucha. A strong green tea from north China so named because the tea leaves are tightly rolled to resemble pellets.

SEMI-FERMENTED—also known as oolong tea. Oolong leaves are semi-fermented before drying to produce a tea halfway between green and black. It is a group of semi-fermented teas with a slight floral aftertaste and they include such teas as:

- **Ti Kwan Yin (Tie Guanyin),** the most popular of oolong teas has the fragrance of orchids.
- **Jasmine** or **Mut Lei Faa (Molihua)**, is a semi-fermented oolong or green tea with jasmine flowers added.

FERMENTED—also known as black tea. The leaves are wilted and bruised by rolling, then fermented and dried.

- **Black Dragon,** a popular brand of black tea.
- **Keemun (Qi Men)**, the most famous of Chinese black teas reputed to be the king of black teas with its smoky flavor and a rosy smell.
- **Bo Lei (Puer)** has an earthy flavor and is a popular tea to accompany dim sum because of its reputed ability to counteract greasy food and lower cholesterol.

OTHER TEAS

SCENTED—some tea leaves are dried with flowers, fruit, or juices.

- **Jasmine Pearl Green Tea,** a green or semi-fermented oolong tea with jasmine flowers with a strong scent of jasmine flowers.
- **Lychee Tea,** a black tea with dried lychee or flavoring.
- **Chrysanthemum Tea,** a green tea mixed with edible dried blossoms.
- **Rose Tea,** a black tea with dried rosebuds.
- **Tisanes,** consists of dried herbs, fruit, and spices but doesn't contain any tea leaves.

SMOKY TEA

- **Lapsang Souchong,** a smoked black tea.

BREWING TEA

Tea is brewed by steeping the loose leaves or a tea bag in boiling water. Fill a pot or kettle with fresh water and bring it to a rolling boil without the tea leaves. Meanwhile, fill the teapot with hot water to warm it. Empty the teapot and measure about one teaspoon of tea leaves for each cup of tea you plan to make. Pour the boiling water directly over the tea leaves; cover and steep 3 to 5 minutes before serving.

For another serving, add more boiling water to the teapot. The second infusion of tea is said to be the best. Green tea requires less steeping time than semi-fermented and black teas. Add more tea leaves to make the tea stronger. More steeping time only makes the tea bitter.

TEA IN DIM SUM RESTAURANTS

Tea is always served with dim sum and with every Chinese meal.

Outside Hawai'i, in the fancier dim sum establishments, a server will ask what type of tea you would like with your food. You may even receive two tea pots: One with the hot tea of your choosing and the other with hot water so you can dilute your tea or drink hot water as your beverage.

In Hawai'i, you probably will be given a basic black tea as the house tea, unless you request a special one for a fee.

As the drinking of tea is as important to dim sum as the food is, it is important to note that it is customary to pour tea for others first before filling one's own cup. To ask for more tea, simply turn over the lid of the teapot when empty to let your server know that you need a refill. After your teacup is being refilled, it is the Cantonese custom to tap your fingers on the table near your cup twice as a sign of thanks.

TAPPING YOUR FINGERS ON THE TABLE TWICE MEANS "THANK YOU"

The legend starts with Chinese Emperor Qian Long who would travel around the country in disguise to see what the commoners were doing. One day, he poured tea for one of his entourage. The staffer wanted to show his gratitude, but could not bow as that would give away the emperor's identity. So he tapped his fingers on the table as a symbol.

Today, there is a practical reason for this gesture as friends who are enjoying yum cha are talking the whole time. The tapping of fingers on the table to say thank you is a way to avoid stopping the conversation.

DIM SUM COMBINATIONS

The types of dim sum are really unlimited, but a few combinations have become popular. After researching and thinking about the choices, here is one observation.

Every dim sum offered is the culmination of three decisions:

1. **Choose your filling**
   - Sweet or Savory Vegetarian—bamboo shoots, black mushrooms, water chestnuts, spinach
   - Pork—fresh or roasted
   - Chicken
   - Shrimp or other seafood
   - Sweetened mashed beans
   - Barbecued sweet pork (char siu)
   - Sausage (lap cheong)
   - Bamboo shoots
   - Water chestnuts
   - Coconut, candied winter melon and peanuts
   - Spinach or garlic chives
   - Or combinations with unlimited options

2. **What covering?**
   - Wheat flour skin (pei) such as for Wonton
   - Wheat starch which is translucent (for the shrimp-filled Har Gow)
   - Bean curd (foo pei or foo jook)
   - Flaky turnover-type pastry (soo)
   - Two types of wheat flour dough for another type of flakiness (for Ma Tai Soo)
   - Rice grains (for pearl balls and shrimp balls)
   - Glutinous rice flour (for sweet and savory Ip Jai)
   - Plain rice flour with wheat starch and tapioca starch (Ham Sui Gok)
   - Soft milk bread that is steamed (Bao)
   - Sweet bread (Baked Bao)

» Tofu (Yeung Dow Foo or Foo Pei)
» None (where the filling is also the cover as with steamed beef meatballs)

3. **How do you want it cooked?**
   » Steamed
   » Baked
   » Deep-fried
   » Shallow pan-fried
   » Braised in sauce
   » Boiled
   » Combinations of the above. For example, turnip cake (Lo Bak Go) is steamed and then pan-fried just before serving. Bean Curd Wrap (Sin Chet Guen)'s filling is boiled, then stir-fried. After it is wrapped with bean curd, it is deep-fried, simmered in sauce, then steamed. In Hawai'i, it is debated which Barbecued Pork Bun (Char Siu Bao, also called manapua) is more popular—steamed or baked? Although many say you can use the same Bao recipe for both cooking methods, the most popular Baked Bao is yellow, sweeter, and more like a brioche bread versus the white slightly sweet steamed variety.

Certain combinations have become popular and others have disappeared. Use this cookbook to try the most popular combinations of fillings, coverings, and cooking style. In any case, going out for yum cha will give you the enjoyment and variety that you may crave.

—Lynette

A good luck banner posted near the front door, inside the home.

Hawai'i's TOP 10 Favorite Dim Sum

People have strong feelings about their favorite dish when they "Yum Cha" or drink tea, meaning eating dim sum, drinking tea, and socializing. In speaking to restaurant owners, managers, and observing the constant flow of foods, here is an unscientific list of what people in Hawai'i order.

SHRIMP DUMPLINGS
Har Gow

MAKES ABOUT 24 DUMPLINGS

The pink shrimp chunks peeking through a translucent, thin wrapper that is steamed to perfection may be the best-selling dim sum around the world. The flavor is mild, but beloved. Har Gow is sold at every restaurant claiming to specialize in dim sum. As Mary Rose Shen says, "if I haven't eaten har gow, I haven't eaten dim sum."

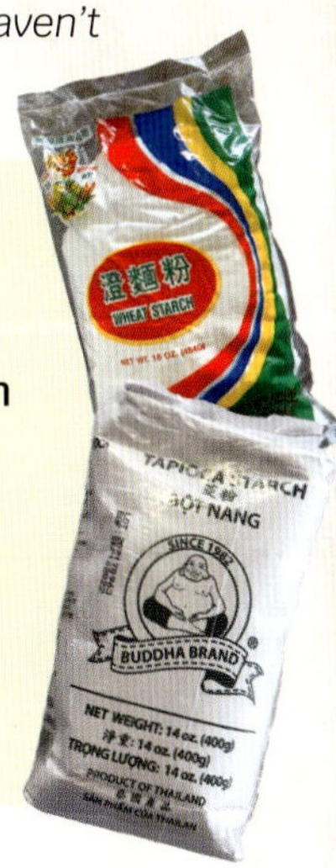

FILLING
- 1 pound raw shrimp, cleaned and chopped
- ¼ pound finely ground pork
- 1 tablespoon minced green onion
- 2 teaspoons soy sauce
- 1 teaspoon salt
- ¼ teaspoon sesame oil
- Dash of white pepper

DOUGH
- 1¼ cups wheat starch
- ¼ cup tapioca starch
- ¼ teaspoon salt
- 1¼ cups boiling water
- 1 teaspoon peanut, vegetable, or canola oil

Combine all the filling ingredients; set aside.

In a medium bowl, combine wheat starch, tapioca starch, and salt; stir to combine. Add boiling water gradually, stirring and mixing well. Add oil. Knead until smooth on surface dusted lightly with wheat starch, adding more if necessary to prevent sticking. Divide dough into thirds; roll each portion into an 8-inch-long cylinder. Cover loosely with slightly damp towel to prevent dough from drying out. Set aside.

Cut each cylinder of dough crosswise into 8 pieces; roll each piece into 3-inch circle on surface lightly dusted with wheat starch. Make seven narrow pleats from edge of dough alongside edge to near center of the circle, each almost overlapping the previous one with final pleats about halfway around the circumference of the dough. Press lightly along the inside of the pleats to flatten them slightly while forming "pocket" within. Spoon a teaspoon of filling into the pocket, keeping it from touching open edge of dough. Pinch edges of dough together firmly to seal. Repeat with remaining wheat starch skins and filling.

Start water boiling in a wok or steamer. Arrange dumplings and place on oiled pans, separating them by at least ½-inch. Steam 8 to 10 minutes over high heat. Repeat in batches, replenishing boiling water as needed. Serve immediately with your favorite sauce (page 170).

VARIATION

SHRIMP DUMPLINGS WITH WATER CHESTNUTS

Ma Tai Har Gow

FILLING

- ½ pound raw shrimp, cleaned and minced
- ¼ cup minced water chestnuts
- 1 tablespoon minced green onion
- 2 teaspoons soy sauce
- 1½ teaspoons salt
- ½ teaspoon minced fresh ginger
- ¼ teaspoon sesame oil

Follow above recipe for wheat starch dough and instructions and use this filling combination.

PORK HASH DUMPLINGS
Siu Mai

MAKES ABOUT 50 DUMPLINGS

Anyone can make these most popular dumplings easily at home. Wonton wrappers or "skins" are available in many markets. If the wrappers are frozen, thaw completely before unwrapping and using them.

FILLING

4 dried black mushrooms, soaked in hot water
1 pound ground pork
½ pound shrimp, peeled, cleaned, and chopped
¼ cup minced green onion
3 tablespoons minced water chestnuts
1 large egg, beaten
1 tablespoon cornstarch
1 teaspoon soy sauce
1 teaspoon salt
¼ teaspoon sugar
¼ teaspoon toasted sesame oil
Dash of white pepper

2 (8-ounce) packages siu mai or wonton wrappers (about 25 wrappers in 8 ounces)
Chinese parsley, goji berry, or pea for garnish

Discard stems from rehydrated mushrooms; mince caps and place in a medium bowl with the remaining filling ingredients; mix together and refrigerate 30 to 60 minutes.

Place 1 tablespoon pork mixture in center of each wrapper. Gather edges of wrapper around filling, leaving tops open. Repeat with the remaining wrappers and filling. Arrange finished dumplings ½-inch apart in lightly greased pan. Top each siu mai with Chinese parsley leaf, goji berry, or pea and place in paper-lined steamer.

Steam over boiling water in steamer for 15 to 20 minutes, replenishing the pot with boiling water as necessary. Serve hot or at room temperature with your favorite sauce (page 170).

Back in the day, the Hawai'i term for Pork Hash was 'ōkole (Hawaiian for buttocks). The term has fallen out of favor.

BARBECUED PORK BUNS

Char Siu Bao

MAKES ABOUT 36 BAO

This has to be one of the most popular dim sums ordered in Hawai'i. Marinated, then roasted pork bits are mixed with sweet seasonings and stuffed into a soft bun that is steamed. Jane Akitake from Maui shares this recipe from her mother, Tue Ngoot Chin. Use her wonderful dough recipe with other fillings too. It is one of the best.

FILLING

- 4 cups diced Char Siu (page 124 or bought)
- 1/4 cup chopped green onions
- 4 tablespoons sugar
- 2 tablespoons hoisin sauce
- 1 tablespoon soy sauce
- 1 tablespoon oyster sauce
- 1 teaspoon salt
- 1/2 teaspoon sesame oil
- 1/2 tablespoons cornstarch combined with 2 to 3 tablespoons tap water

DOUGH

- 6 1/2 cups all-purpose flour
- 1 cup sugar
- 1/2 cup shortening
- 1 cup 2% milk, substitute any milk, warmed to about 110°F
- 1 cup warm water, about 110°F
- 1 package (2 1/4 teaspoons) active dry or rapid rise yeast

PREPARE THE FILLING:

Start to heat all filling ingredients (except cornstarch and water) in a skillet over medium heat for about 5 minutes. Mix cornstarch and water thoroughly. Add to pan and cook for about 2 to 3 minutes until cornstarch has thickened slightly. Remove from heat and let cool completely. Keep refrigerated until ready to shape the bao.

MAKE THE BAO:

In a mixing bowl, combine flour and sugar then cut in shortening. Set aside.

Mix together warm milk and warm water then dissolve yeast into the milk mixture. Add dry ingredients to milk mixture in a standing mixer with a dough hook for 5 minutes. Alternatively, knead by hand for 5 minutes. Cover with a clean dish towel and let rise in a warm and not windy part of your kitchen or in the oven (do not turn on oven) until doubled or tripled in volume, about two to four hours.

Punch down dough and knead for 1 to 2 minutes. Cut into 36 portions. Round one into a ball. Form a flat circle and add 1 tablespoon of the filling. Pleat and twist to seal and form a small knot on top. Place each bao on a 3-inch square of freezer wrap or parchment paper. Let rise in a warm area or return to unheated oven about 15 to 20 minutes.

Place in steamer and steam on high heat approximately 8 to 10 minutes. Remove from steamer and place on rack to cool. Serve or cool completely and freeze.

REHEATING INSTRUCTIONS:

- **Frozen:** Cover with a slightly damp paper towel and microwave for 30 to 60 seconds.
- **Refrigerated:** Cover with a slightly damp paper towel and microwave for 30 seconds or less.
- Repeat 10 seconds or so, as needed.

STEAMER:

Steam bao for 5 to 8 minutes. Do not over-heat, since the bao may get chewy.

Bao are ready when bread springs back after being pressed.

STEAMED ROLLS

Cheung Fun

MAKES ABOUT 8 ROLLS

These tender, thin rolls are delicate and can be eaten without any protein—just with a sweet soy sauce mixture or oyster sauce. Or steamed scallops or shrimp can be added in or on top. Other favorites include char siu, beef, or minced dried shrimp. Alternatively, this recipe from great Honolulu home cook June Kam Tong of Popo's Kitchen cookbooks, uses cake flour to simulate the tender rice flour rolls. It works as well and is delicious and is presented here.

1 cup Swans Down cake flour
¼ cup oil, plus more to oil the pans
2 tablespoons wheat starch
¼ teaspoon salt

Fillings of your choice:
chopped green onions, minced dried shrimp, chopped char siu, steamed shrimp, steamed scallops, etc.

In a bowl, mix flour, oil, wheat starch, salt, and 1⅓ cup water. Start a steamer on high. Oil an 8-inch cake pan. Mix flour mixture thoroughly. When steamer is ready, stir flour mixture again and pour ¼ cup into greased pan.

Prepare a large pan with cool water for use later. Steam on high for 3 to 5 minutes until roll is cooked and has bubbles. Cool in large pan with water for about 3 minutes. This cooling allows you to easily remove the Cheung Fun. Start another batch in an oiled pan in the steamer. Sprinkle cooled cheung fun with small amount (about 2 teaspoons) of filling. Using your finger, gently roll the steamed fun and lift up away from the pan so the fun is smooth. Once more than halfway, you can rotate pan and roll the opposite way. The end result is a soft smooth roll. Serve as is or with a sweetened soy sauce (page 173). Cover with plastic wrap if not serving right away.

Eimi Zecha fondly remembers when she was a young girl in Hong Kong that a vendor would ring a bell to signal that fresh cheung fun noodles were for sale on the street. People would run down to savor the plain, tender noodles with just a sweet soy sauce over the slippery "noodles."

HALF MOON DUMPLINGS
Gok Jai (Fan Gwo)

MAKES ABOUT 24 DUMPLINGS

These pork and vegetable dumplings are made from wheat starch, which makes them translucent when steamed. Usually shaped like a half moon with the rounded edge sealed with a twisted design, a nickname is "half-moon." In Hawai'i, they are also called pepeiao, which means ear in the Hawaiian language, because you could imagine that you are seeing a large ear. Another name it's known as in Hawai'i is Gok Jai, outside of Hawai'i, it is called Fan Gwo. This involves a little more preparation to make the wrapper rather than buy a wheat flour one, but it is well worth the effort.

DOUGH

- 1¼ cups wheat starch (doong mein fun)
- ¼ cup tapioca starch
- ¼ teaspoon salt
- 1¼ cups boiling water
- 1 teaspoon peanut, vegetable, or canola oil

FILLING

- 1 clove garlic, mashed
- 1 teaspoon minced fresh ginger
- 1 tablespoon peanut, vegetable, or canola oil
- 1 cup ground pork
- ½ cup minced dried shrimp
- 1 tablespoon soy sauce
- 2 teaspoons sugar
- 1 large dried mushroom, soaked in hot water 30 minutes, minced
- 1 tablespoon minced green onion
- ⅓ cup chopped bamboo shoots
- ½ cup chopped char siu
- ⅓ cup minced water chestnuts
- 1 tablespoon chopped Chinese parsley

Peanut, vegetable, or canola oil for tops of dumplings

Delicacies at Char Hung Sut

In a medium bowl, combine wheat starch, tapioca starch, and salt; stir to combine. Add boiling water gradually, stirring and mixing well. Knead until smooth on surface dusted lightly with wheat starch, adding more if necessary to prevent sticking. Divide dough into thirds; roll each portion into an 8-inch cylinder. Cover loosely with slightly damp paper towel to prevent dough from drying out. Set aside.

Boiling water is crucial to achieving the texture of the wrapper.

To prepare filling, stir-fry garlic and ginger in hot oil in wok or large skillet; add pork and stir-fry 1 minute. Add dried shrimp, soy sauce, sugar, mushrooms, green onion, bamboo shoots; remove from heat and add char siu, water chestnuts, and Chinese parsley; mix well and set aside to cool.

Pinch off small pieces of dough; roll into a ball then flatten out into a circle and roll out into thin 3-inch circles. Fill half a circle with a teaspoonful of filling. Fold over the other half to form a half moon. Pinch edges together by crimping it like you would pies, with a twist to make an attractive design. Brush top of each dumpling with peanut, vegetable, or canola oil. Arrange in a greased steamer and steam 15 minutes.

Serve with the dipping sauce of your choice (page 170).

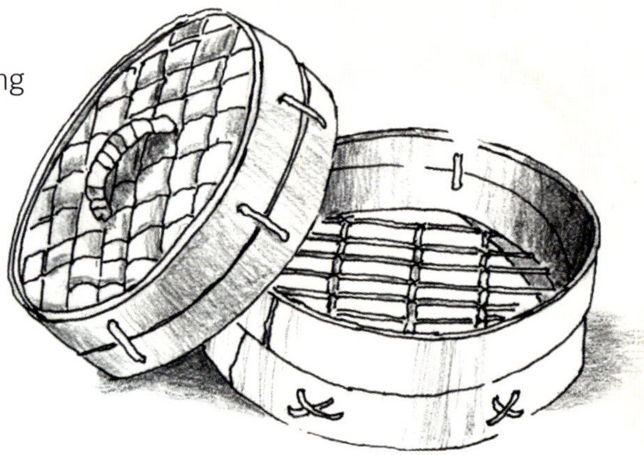

STEAMED AND PAN-FRIED TURNIP CAKE

Lo Bak Go

At dim sum restaurants, one of the most anticipated carts has a small heated unit to grill foods. Delicate steamed turnip cakes are pan-fried to warm them and to achieve a crunchy exterior. Plain rice is milled into flour to provide the batter for the savory sausage bits mixed with the mild-flavored turnip. Half of the turnip is cut into sticks to garner more of the turnip texture and the remainder is grated. Michelle Cheung was generous to share this delicious recipe with Charlene Lo Chan, who shared it with me.

- **1½ Chinese sausages (lap cheong)**
- **3 large dried black mushrooms, soaked in hot water 30 minutes**
- **1½ cups long turnip cut in ¼ × ¼ × 1-inch sticks**
- **1½ cups grated long turnip**
- **Vegetable oil to coat two 8-inch baking pans and for frying**
- **½ teaspoon kosher salt**
- **8 ounces plain rice flour (jeen mai fan) also called sharp rice flour, <u>not</u> glutinous rice flour (no mai fan, mochiko)**
- **Chinese parsley or minced green onions for garnish**

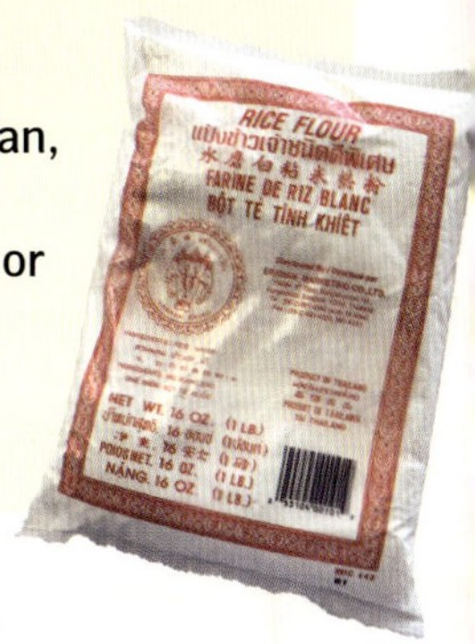

In a sauce pan, put sausage in enough water to cover and cook on medium-high for 5 minutes. Peel and discard sausage skin, if preferred and finely chop. Set aside.

Keep mushroom liquid, discard stems and finely chop mushroom caps.

In a sauce pan, cook sausage and mushrooms with about 3 tablespoons of mushroom liquid over medium heat for 5 minutes.

Peel turnip and cut half into ¼ × ¼ × 1-inch sticks. Roughly grate the other half. Cook all in a saucepan with about 1 cup water over medium heat until turnip is translucent, about 5 minutes. Do not drain liquid.

Mix salt and rice flour in a bowl with the cooked turnip and liquid. Keep adding any remaining mushroom liquid and additional water until the mixture is thin like runny pancake batter. That could be as much as 3/4 cup of liquid.

Using a paper towel, oil two 8-inch round baking pans. Divide the mushroom and sausage mixture equally in both pans. Pour the rice and turnip mixture over and spread evenly. Steam for 50 minutes. Cool. Cut into square or rectangle pieces. Fry both sides until crispy, about 5 minutes on medium high. Serve with soy sauce, oyster sauce, or one of the sauces (page 170). Garnish with Chinese parsley or minced green onions.

VARIATION

STEAMED AND PAN-FRIED TURNIP CAKE WITH SHRIMP

Soak 1/8 cup dried shrimp in hot water until soft. Chop into smaller pieces and add to the batter.

BLACK BEAN SPARERIBS

Dow See Pai Gwat

MAKES 4 SERVINGS

Many people enjoy the "challenge" of eating succulent meat off the bone. The unique flavor of dow see (fermented black beans, Chinese-style) mashed with sugar, ginger, a type of liquor, and garlic is a classic combination with the sweetness of pork spareribs.

1 pound pork spareribs, cut into 1-inch lengths

SAUCE

¼ cup soy sauce
2 tablespoons fermented black beans (dow see), rinsed and mashed
1 tablespoon cornstarch
1 tablespoon Shaoxing wine, substitute dry sherry
2 teaspoons brown sugar
1 teaspoon grated fresh ginger
1 clove garlic, minced

Chopped green onions or Chinese parsley leaves for garnish

Place spareribs in a heat-resistant dish.

Combine sauce ingredients and mix well. Pour over spareribs and mix until spareribs are coated.

Place in steamer; cover and steam over medium heat until done, about 40 to 45 minutes. Some people prefer the ribs to have a chew to them, rather than "falling off the bone." If that is the case, start checking the spareribs for doneness at 30 minutes.

BRAISED CHICKEN FEET

Fung Zaau (Phoenix Claws)

MAKES ABOUT 6 SERVINGS AS AN APPETIZER

This dish is one for which people have strong feelings. It brings up repulsion or craving. Enough people order this to place chicken feet on the top 10 list. There is no meat here, just chewy cartilage flavored with a complex sauce. This recipe has a bit of hotness from the chili bean sauce. It is said that the collagen is great for your complexion. Chinese enjoy texture as another dimension to taste. Chicken feet are valued for their chewy texture. At most Hawaiʻi restaurants, the dish is served tender, almost falling off the bone. However, one friend from Hong Kong tells me that Tim Ho Wan restaurant serves it the way Hong Kong people like it—a bit chewy, not too tender. Restaurants may call these Phoenix Claws; a fancy name for chicken feet.

1 pound chicken feet, about 11 to 13
3 cups water
2 inches ginger, peeled and sliced
½ cup vegetable oil, or more depending on the size of your pan

SAUCE

3 tablespoons soy sauce
3 tablespoons Shaoxing wine, substitute dry sherry
2 tablespoons oyster sauce
3 cloves garlic, minced
2 teaspoons chili bean sauce (dou ban jang)
1 teaspoon ground white pepper
1 teaspoon sugar
½ teaspoon Chinese Five Spice powder

Wash and clean chicken feet. Using a knife or scissors, cut off claws. In a large pot, heat 3 cups water and ginger. When water boils, add chicken feet and boil for 10 minutes. Discard ginger. Drain and pat dry and refrigerate overnight on paper towels, uncovered to drain all water. When chicken feet are drier, there is less splattering when deep fried.

Add enough oil so there is ½-inch of oil in a deep pot. Heat the oil to about 350°F. Fry batches of chicken feet for 5 minutes, watching out for splattering oil. Remove and complete batches. In a Dutch oven, mix cooked chicken feet with sauce ingredients. Cook on medium-low heat covered, stirring every 10 to 15 minutes, until tender, about 1 hour. Add water if needed. There is no need to thicken the sauce as the collagen from the chicken feet is a natural thickener. Serve over Seasoned Peanuts (page 84).

BEAN CURD WRAP
Sin Chet Kuen

MAKES ABOUT 14

Almost every restaurant offers their version of a tasty dim sum wrapped in bean curd wrap (foo pei or foo jook); another form of tofu made from cooked soy beans. The fillings vary from only vegetables to almost all meat; the only common factor is the texture of the wrapping. Dried tofu sheets (foo jook) cannot be used in this method. Those are good to add to soups or jook. Refrigerated or frozen foo pei (tofu skins) should be bought for this favorite dish.

While appearing simple, bean curd wrap dumplings showcase how the Chinese use many cooking methods to create one dish. This recipe boils, then stir-fries the fillings. Then braises them after the fillings are rolled into a wrap. They are steamed before being served on your table.

FILLING

1 pound ground pork
1 Chinese sausage (lap cheong), minced
1 tablespoon vegetable or canola oil
½ cup minced onion
⅛ pound dried shrimp, soaked in water and minced
¼ pound bamboo shoots, minced
1 teaspoon cornstarch
1 tablespoon water
½ teaspoon salt
¼ teaspoon white pepper

COVERING

2 packages frozen or refrigerated bean curd wrap (foo pei, foo jook)*

BRAISING SAUCE

3 cups chicken broth, divided
2 tablespoons cornstarch
1 tablespoon oyster sauce
1 teaspoon peanut, vegetable, or canola oil
1 teaspoon sugar
1 teaspoon salt

(continued on the next page)

THE DAY BEFORE

Prepare the filling by bringing 2 cups of water to boil in a wok or large sauce pan. When water has boiled, add ground pork; cook until color changes, under 1 minute. Remove pork and set aside. Add minced sausage to the hot water and cook for 1 minute. Drain and set aside sausage with the cooked pork. Wash wok.

Add 1 tablespoon oil and heat on high. Add dried shrimp and bamboo shoots and cook for 1 minute. Add in pork and sausage and cook another minute. Mix 1 teaspoon with 1 tablespoon water and add to mixture with salt and pepper; cook until cornstarch has thickened, 1 to 2 minutes. Remove from wok and cool. Cover and refrigerate overnight.

Defrost bean curd wrap if frozen. Cut into 16 triangle shapes 9½ × 9½ × 12½ inches. Set aside and cover with a moist paper towel.

Divide filling into 16 portions. Place one wrap on the table with the widest side facing you. Add one portion of the filling in a log shape about 1 inch away from the bottom of the wrap and centered. The finished roll will measure 5½ inches long and about 2 inches wide. Fold both sides of the wrap over the filling and roll it upwards. Wet your finger with water and run it along the final edges of the wrap, fold and seal. Set aside and repeat folding the wrap until done.

Mix ¼ cup of the chicken broth with cornstarch until dissolved. In a wok over medium-high heat, add the braising liquid of cornstarch mixture, remaining chicken broth, oyster sauce, oil, sugar, and salt. Bring to a boil. Reduce to medium heat and cook for 3 minutes. In batches, place bean curd wraps into braising sauce and cook for 3 minutes. Remove from wok. Repeat until you finish.

Refrigerate and store for up to a few days. Or place two finished wraps on a plate, cover with braising sauce and steam over high heat for 5 minutes. Serve immediately.

*Dried sheets of bean curd (foo jook) cannot be used for this recipe; they are too brittle. They are used in soup and porridge (jook). Different brands contain varying amounts. Allow for 14 large triangles.

CUSTARD TARTS
Dan Tat

MAKES ABOUT 24 TARTS

Every Chinese dim sum restaurant offers these delicate custard tarts, which my grandchildren love to have for dessert. The shells bake to a delicate flakiness.

—Muriel

PASTRY
1¼ cups all-purpose flour
1 tablespoon sugar
Pinch salt
⅓ cup lard or shortening
¼ cup ice water

FILLING
2 large eggs, beaten
⅓ cup sugar
⅓ cup milk
¼ teaspoon vanilla

(continued on the next page)

To prepare pastry, whisk together flour, sugar, and salt. Cut in lard or shortening using pastry blender or fork until mixture resembles crumbs the size of small peas. Drizzle with ice water; tossing briskly with fork, until dough barely holds together. Add a few drops more of water, if necessary, but do not overwork the dough. Press together to form a ball then press into round, flat disks. Wrap in plastic and refrigerate until chilled, about 30 to 45 minutes.

On lightly floured surface, roll dough to 1/8-inch thickness. Using a cookie cutter, cut out twelve 3½-inch circles, re-rolling scraps. Fit, without stretching, into fluted tart or muffin tins, pressing the dough lightly into the bottoms. Stuff each with crumpled foil. Refrigerate 30 minutes.

Bake at 425°F for 6 to 8 minutes or until pastry shells start to turn light brown. Remove foil and cool.

To make the filling, whisk ingredients together in a medium bowl; let mixture rest 10 minutes; skim off any bubbles then pour milk mixture slowly into tart shells until three-fourths full.

Bake at 325°F for 30 to 35 minutes or until knife inserted in center comes out clean and the crusts are lightly browned.

Cool 5 to 10 minutes. Loosen tarts from pan using knife or small spatula. Best served warm but may also be served at room temperature or chilled.

Dumplings

When you ask someone to "yum cha" or drink tea, they are expecting dim sum type foods along with tea and good conversation. There are no hard rules, but in general they expect dumplings.

Dumplings are small bites of food. Perhaps you can finish one of the morsels in one or two bites. They usually are covered in a wrapper of some kind that can vary from the common wheat flour dough to the translucent wheat starch or wheat starch–tapioca starch combination to dried bean curd to a chewy covering of glutinous rice flour.

In Hawai'i, we love our dim sum. When workers get promoted, they take dim sum to the job site for everyone. When we visit the neighbor islands, we make people happy by bringing them Manapua.

There are many, many combinations of fillings, coverings, and cooking methods to result in delicious dumplings. Here are a few recipes for you to enjoy making at home.

FRIED PORK AND SHRIMP DUMPLINGS
Gau Gee

MAKES ABOUT 36 DUMPLINGS

At any Hawai'i potluck you attend, chances are good that someone will bring gau gee to the party. It is easy to make at home or ordered from a restaurant by itself, or on top of stir-fried noodles. Actually, the fillings for wonton, pork hash dumplings, and gau gee can be switched interchangeably. What enables it to be called Gau Gee is the shape—its rectangle shape and that it is deep-fried. Some restaurants omit the shrimp, for cost reasons and because some customers are allergic. For a richer, fuller taste, include the shrimp and the minced mushroom.

FILLING

Optional: 2 dried black mushrooms, soaked in hot water for 30 minutes
½ pound ground pork
¼ pound raw shrimp, peeled, deveined and minced
¼ cup minced green onions
8 water chestnuts, minced
1 teaspoon oyster sauce
½ teaspoon salt
½ teaspoon soy sauce
¼ teaspoon white pepper

2 (8-ounce) packages square wonton wrappers (about 25 wrappers in 8 ounces)
1 quart vegetable or canola oil for frying

If using mushrooms, remove stems and mince. In a large bowl, combine remaining filling ingredients. Mix well and divide filling into 36 portions. Fill a small bowl with water. Place wrapper in hand. In the center, place one portion of filling. Using your finger, wet half of the wrapper and fold over into a rectangle. Press to seal. Repeat until done.

Heat oil to 365°F and deep fry in batches until golden brown and crisp. Drain on paper towels. Serve hot or at room temperature with a sauce of your choice (page 170).

PORK DUMPLINGS
Wonton

MAKES ABOUT 48 DUMPLINGS

Wonton can be eaten in several ways: floating in a bowl of soup, poached and served with a spoonful of hot chili sauce, or deep-fried and served with sweet sour sauce.

FILLING

- ½ pound ground pork, or ground chicken or turkey
- ¼ pound raw shrimp, shelled and deveined, chopped
- ¼ cup minced water chestnuts
- 3 tablespoons minced green onion
- 2 tablespoons chopped Chinese parsley
- 1 tablespoon soy sauce
- 1 large egg, beaten
- 1 teaspoon cornstarch
- 1 teaspoon oyster sauce
- 1 teaspoon sugar
- ¼ teaspoon salt

- 2 (8-ounce) packages wonton wrappers
- 1 quart vegetable or canola oil for deep-frying

Mix filling ingredients.

Place about a teaspoon of the mixture in center of a wonton wrapper. Moisten edges with water; fold in half to form triangle; press to seal and flip back to meet the fold. Pull the other two opposite corners together; twist under; moisten tips and press together to seal.

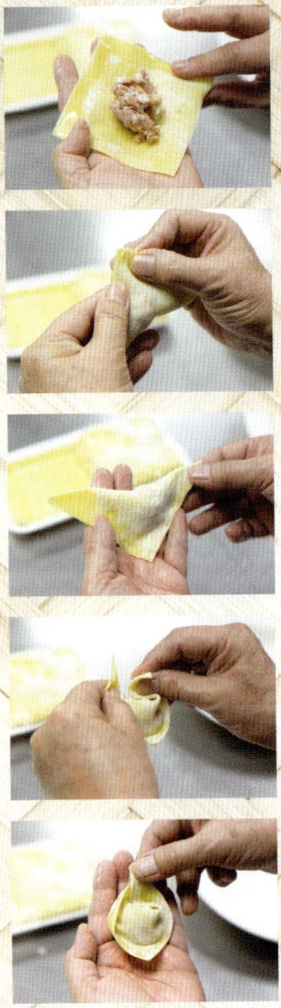

Fry in oil heated to 365°F until lightly browned. Drain on paper towels or metal rack. Serve with sauce of choice (page 170).

Or boil in batches until wontons float for 2 minutes. Drain and serve with a dipping sauce or add the cooked wontons into soup.

VARIATIONS

- **Ham wonton:** substitute ham for ground pork.
- **SPAM® wonton:** substitute canned SPAM® luncheon meat for ground pork, add chopped onion.
- **Kālua pig-kim chee wonton:** chop kālua pig and drain kim chee, omit ground pork.
- **Poultry wonton:** substitute ground chicken or turkey for pork.
- **Create your own favorite wonton:** combine extra firm tofu with other vegetables, other meats with vegetables, etc. Add 1/2 teaspoon sesame oil if using tofu.

Note: Wonton may be made ahead and frozen individually. After 30 minutes, the frozen dumplings can be combined and stored in a plastic bag. Boil while frozen or thaw before frying. Or, they may be fried earlier, then frozen and reheated before serving. Wonton wrappers are available in most markets and at Asian noodle factories.

SEAFOOD SIU MAI

Hoi Seen Siu Mai

MAKES ABOUT 30 DUMPLINGS

Wonton wrappers may be used to hold a variety of fillings—chicken, shrimp, pork, scallops, fishcake, and more. The dumplings can either be steamed or fried and served with a dipping sauce of your choice.

FILLING

½ pound medium raw shrimp, shelled and deveined
½ pound scallops
½ pound ground pork
1 tablespoon minced fresh ginger
2 tablespoons minced fresh Chinese parsley leaves
2 tablespoons minced green onion
1 teaspoon rice vinegar
1 teaspoon toasted sesame oil
1 large egg, slightly beaten
Salt and pepper to taste
2 teaspoons cornstarch
Juice of ½ lemon

1½ (8-ounce) packages wonton or siu mai wrappers (about 25 wrappers per package)
Canola or vegetable oil for brushing steamer
Cabbage for lining steamer or individual pieces of parchment paper
Minced green onions, defrosted green peas, crab, or fish eggs for garnish

To make filling, finely mince shrimp and scallops; combine in medium bowl with remaining filling ingredients. Mix well.

To make siu mai, fill centers of wonton wrappers with 1 tablespoon filling. Moisten edges of wrappers, gather edges around filling, and pinch the sides together with fingers to form pleated cups. Do not enclose filling, leaving the top open. Slightly tap the dumpling on the tables to flatten the bottom. Repeat with remaining wrappers and filling.

Top each siu mai with a colorful contrast such as green onions, one green pea or orange fish eggs and place in slightly oiled steamer lined with cabbage or parchment paper. Steam siu mai for 10 to 15 minutes.

Garnish with green onions and serve with soy sauce or dipping sauce of choice (page 170).

Tip: A 10-inch bamboo steamer will accommodate about 12 siu mai.

Variation: ¼ cup tobiko (flying fish eggs) as a colorful topping.

SOUP DUMPLINGS
Sui Gow

MAKES ABOUT 30

Sui Gow means soup dumplings and they are not always offered in Hawai'i restaurants. They are the delicious cousin to wonton; larger in size and always served in soup. Wontons can be boiled and served without soup, or fried. If you are shopping at a Chinese noodle factory, they will sell you sui gow wrappers, which are the same texture and thickness as the "skins" for wonton, but are larger and round. Gyoza wrappers are smaller. Mandoo wrappers are thicker than you would want. If you cannot find the specific wrappers, use gyoza wrappers or buy wonton wrappers and cut off the corners to make them round.

¼ cup (2 to 3 dried mushrooms) chopped black mushrooms, rehydrated and stems removed
½ cup ground pork, substitute ground chicken
½ cup raw shrimp, peeled, deveined and chopped
¼ cup chopped water chestnuts or jicama
¼ cup chopped won bok cabbage, substitute bok choy or cabbage
¼ cup chopped green onions
1 tablespoon chopped Chinese parsley
1 tablespoon cornstarch
1 tablespoon soy sauce
1 tablespoon Shaoxing wine or dry sherry
½ teaspoon sesame oil
½ teaspoon salt
¼ teaspoon white pepper
12 ounces sui gow pei (30 wheat dough wraps for soup dumplings), substitute gyoza or round wonton wrappers

Soak dried mushrooms in hot water for at least 30 minutes. Chop the caps into small pieces. Discard stems and in a large mixing bowl, combine all ingredients except the wraps. Fill a small dish with water. Place 1 tablespoon filling into a wrap. Using your finger, wet half of the "skin" and fold over. Press the dumpling closed. Repeat until completed. Cook in batches in boiling water until cooked, about 5 minutes. Serve in a soup or broth of your choice. A side dip of spicy or vinegar sauce can be prepared (page 170). These dumplings are best fresh; not frozen.

BEEF DUMPLINGS
Ngau Yuk Siu Mai

MAKES ABOUT 18 DUMPLINGS

Since people are familiar with pork dumplings rather than beef, this recipe should be a nice alternative. In southern China, the word for meat is assumed to mean pork. Pigs were much more prevalent in the south; the north had more sheep and cattle.

FILLING

3 dried black mushrooms, soaked in hot water 30 minutes
½ pound ground beef
½ cup minced bamboo shoots
¼ cup minced green onions
1 teaspoon soy sauce
1 teaspoon salt
1 teaspoon toasted sesame oil
½ teaspoon Shaoxing wine, substitute dry sherry

1 (8-ounce) package round wonton, siu mai, or gyoza wrappers (Mandoo wrappers will be thicker, so are not recommended.)

Discard mushroom stems and mince caps. Combine filling ingredients. Mix until well-blended. Divide filling into 18 portions. Place one portion filling in center of each circle of dough; fold over into semi-circle. Pinch edges together into ½-inch wide ledge and form scroll or rope design along edges.

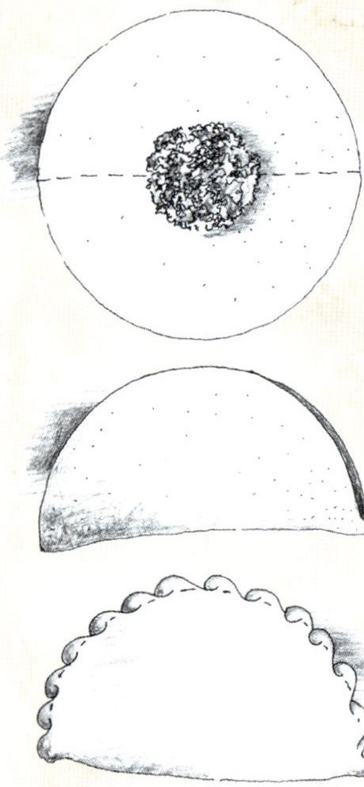

Brush oil on a metal steamer, on vegetable leaves or pieces of parchment on a bamboo steamer. Place dumplings so they do not touch each other. Steam 30 to 35 minutes.

POTSTICKERS
Guo Tip

MAKES ABOUT 36 POTSTICKERS

Alex Hsieh shares his mother (Florence Tiok-Kun Yap)'s filling recipe for many dishes: Potstickers, siu mai, with an egg wrap, wonton, and just eaten by itself. Potstickers combine two different cooking methods to achieve the its chewy, yet tender wrapping. First, the dumpling is pan-fried in a bit of oil, then after browned, water or broth is added and the dumplings finish cooking by steaming. You can't stop eating these. Especially good with a dipping sauce (page 170).

FILLING

1 pound ground pork
1 cup shrimp, chopped (about ½ pound)
½ cup finely chopped bamboo shoots
4 dried black mushrooms, rehydrated and chopped
3 stalks green onion, chopped (about ¾ cup)
4½ tablespoons water
1 large egg, beaten
1½ tablespoon soy sauce
1½ teaspoon cornstarch
1 teaspoon sesame oil
¾ teaspoon salt
⅛ teaspoon ground black pepper

2 (8-ounce) packages round wonton or gyoza wrappers (mandoo wrappers are thicker, so are not recommended)
Vegetable or canola oil

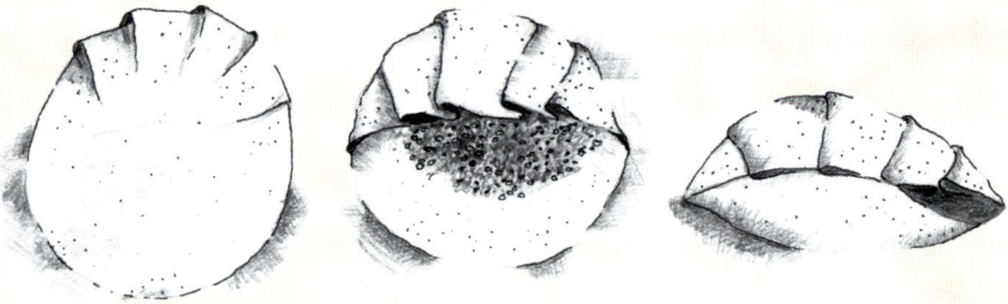

Combine filling ingredients. Place about 2 teaspoons filling in center of round wrapper. Wet edges with water and fold in half and seal tightly. The dumplings will be in a shape of a half moon. Heat about 2 tablespoons oil in skillet and fry potstickers in batches uncovered on both sides until they are golden brown. Carefully add 1/4 cup water to pan and cover. Steam potstickers until they are cooked through, about 5 minutes. Serve hot or at room temperature with a dipping sauce (page 170).

SAVORY STUFFED GLUTINOUS RICE FLOUR DOUGHNUTS

Ham Sui Gok

MAKES ABOUT 16 DUMPLINGS

June Kam Tong of Popo's Kitchen *cookbooks is generous to share her tasty recipe for the savory version of Jin Dui. If you like the chewiness of the sweet Chinese doughnut, you will enjoy the same fried outer covering. This version is filled with seasoned minced pieces of roast pork, char siu, and dried shrimp.*

FILLING

½ cup minced roast pork
½ cup minced char siu
¼ cup minced dried shrimp*
¼ cup chopped green onions
¼ cup chopped Chinese parsley
1 tablespoon oyster sauce

COVERING

¾ cup brown sugar
1¼ cup hot water, plus more as needed
⅛ cup mashed boiled or canned yams
2 tablespoons Shaoxing wine or whiskey
1 pound glutinous rice flour (no mai fun), also called mochiko
½ cup white or black sesame seeds
1 quart vegetable or canola oil

In a large bowl, mix the filling ingredients thoroughly. Set aside. In a bowl, combine brown sugar, water, yams, and whiskey. Mix until sugar is dissolved. Set aside. Place flour in a large bowl. Add the sugar mixture and stir until dough is cool enough to be handled. Add more flour or water as needed to get a texture you are able to hold. Pinch dough into balls the size of a golf ball. Flatten dough and form a small well. Place a small amount of filling in the center. Seal edges and form a ball. Roll each ball in sesame seeds and set aside.

Heat oil in a wok until it is 350°F. Drop in a very small piece of dough. If it sizzles, it is ready. Remove test piece of dough.

Reduce heat to low and place 5 balls into the oil. Using a kitchen spider, roll the balls in the oil until they turn a light brown. Increase heat to 365°F and press the doughnuts against the side of the wok with the spider. Continue to rotate and press the doughnuts. They will double in size. When doughnuts are brown, remove from oil and let drain on metal racks or paper towels. Repeat until done. Eat that day.

*Chinese dried shrimp are tough. Either soak them in hot water for 30 minutes (save the flavorful soaking liquid) before chopping or chop finely in a food processor. In this recipe, you just want the flavor of dried shrimp; they do not need to be kept in chunks.

WATER CHESTNUT AND PORK PASTRY

Ma Tai Soo

MAKES 16 PASTRIES

Ma tai means water chestnut and soo refers to a flaky pastry that is covering the filling. One of the best ma tai soos was sold in Chinatown at the popular Char Hung Sut, now shuttered. The outside pastry was strong and could hold a flavorful mix of sweet char siu, mushrooms, and vegetables. Here is our attempt to imitate the memorable dim sum of CHS. Two different doughs are combined to create the flaky layers. The good news is these are easily frozen after baking so you can always have some in your freezer.

FILLING

½ cup diced dried black mushrooms, soaked in hot water for 30 minutes, stems discarded
1 cup diced char siu
½ cup diced dried shrimp, soaked in hot water
½ cup diced water chestnuts
½ cup diced bamboo shoots
¼ cup grated raw turnip, drained
¼ cup chopped green onions
¼ cup chopped Chinese parsley
1 teaspoon soy sauce
1 teaspoon sugar
1 teaspoon sesame oil
½ teaspoon salt

In a wok or skillet, combine filling ingredients on medium heat and cook until all ingredients are heated, about 5 minutes. Check that turnip is cooked. Drain if there is excess liquid. Divide the mixture into 16 servings (approximately 2 tablespoons) and set aside.

DOUGH #1

1 cup all-purpose flour
½ cup shortening

Blend Dough #1 separately, divide into 16 equal parts and set aside.

DOUGH #2

2 cups all-purpose flour
¾ cup water
¼ cup shortening
2 tablespoons sugar

Blend Dough #2 separately, divide into 16 equal parts and set aside.

Take one piece of Dough #1 and combine into one piece of Dough #2, wrapping Dough #2 around Dough #1 into a ball. It doesn't have to be perfect. Between two pieces of parchment paper or plastic wrap, use a small rolling pin and roll the ball into a long narrow strip. Don't worry about irregularities in the color of the blended dough. Beginning at one narrow end, roll the incorporated dough strip into a narrow tight log. Curl one end of the log under the dough and the other end of the log on top of the dough into an off-centered ball. Repeat until all the dough is incorporated in 16 off-centered balls.

(continued on the next page)

ASSEMBLY

1 large egg, beaten

Red food coloring

Preheat oven to 375°F. Roll each dough ball between parchment or plastic wrap into a flat round disk about 1/4-inch thick. Shape your hand as if you're holding a tall glass and place the disk flat in the crook of your thumb and index finger. Indent a divot without puncturing the disk. Fill the divot with about 2 tablespoons of filling. Gently form the edges of the dough to create a bag with a flat bottom without breaking any part of the dough. Flip the pastry over to lay flat on a parchment-lined cookie sheet so the crimping is not visible and a nice smooth bulb appears. Using a pastry brush, paint the top of the "ball" with beaten egg, let dry for about 15 minutes so the red food coloring does not bleed. In the center of each pastry, dot once with red food coloring using the end of a round, wooden chopstick.

Bake at 375°F for 15 minutes. Rotate the cookie sheet and bake 15 more minutes or until golden brown. Cool for 5 minutes before serving at room temperature. Serve with Chinese mustard and soy sauce or red chili paste and soy sauce.

These are easily frozen individually in foil or plastic wrap. Defrost and bake at 300°F for 20 minutes to refresh. Do not use a microwave as the texture will not be flaky.

Robert "Buggy" McFarlane said he loved the crust of CHS's ma tai soo. "The bottom crust was thicker than the other parts. So delicious."

Bao (Buns), Rolls, and Bread

Steamed or Baked Buns (Bao) are one of the most popular foods in Hawai'i. Many mothers will feed their babies the soft Steamed Bao. The Steamed Bao is generally white in color, while the baked varieties usually include egg so are more yellow. Both breads are slightly sweet, which adds to their appeal in sugar-loving Hawai'i.

Northern Chinese breads are also appreciated such as the plain steamed bread called Mantou, or Fried Green Onion Cake (Chun Yau Bang) or the delicate Mandarin Pancakes which are the perfect companion to Roast Duck or a Meat and Vegetable Stir-fry (Mu Shu). Fried Spring Rolls are always enjoyed at parties.

BUN DOUGH FOR STEAMING
Bao

MAKES 16 TO 18 BUNS

The popular bread we call bao is white from milk and all-purpose flour and sweet from sugar. Shortening or lard is an ingredient. Steaming bao results in a delicate, soft bun that is treasured in dim sum offerings.

3 cups all-purpose flour
1/4 cup shortening
1/4 cup sugar, divided in half
1 1/8 teaspoons active dry yeast
1/3 cup warm water
2/3 cup warm whole milk (substitute water, coconut milk, or soy milk)

Put flour into large bowl and use a butter knife or pastry cutter to cut into shortening. Stir in 1/8 cup sugar.

In a separate, small bowl combine remaining 1/8 cup sugar with yeast and warm water (about 110°F) then stir until yeast is dissolved.

Combine flour mixture, yeast mixture, and the warm milk (about 110°F) until a ball forms. If the dough is too sticky, add flour gradually. Transfer dough to floured surface; knead until smooth and elastic, about 10 to 12 minutes. Or use a standing mixer. Place dough in bowl and use dough hook to mix for 10 minutes. Place dough in a greased bowl, cover, and let rise until dough is doubled. If your kitchen is windy, place bowl in an unheated oven. Place a mug with boiling water in the oven next to the bowl to create the slightly warm temperature for the dough to rise. It may take 1 or 2 hours for dough to double in size.

When dough is ready, punch down and roll into cylinder shape about 2 inches in diameter and 16 inches long. Cut cylinder into 16 to 18 portions. Flatten each piece with your hands and roll into a disk about 3-inches in diameter and 1/2-inch thick.

Place 1 tablespoon of desired filling in center of dough. Form into buns by pulling dough up and around filling. Repeat with remaining pieces of dough and filling. Pinch to seal seams. Place on squares of parchment paper if steaming, or on lightly greased baking pan, if baking. Let rest 20 to 30 minutes.

To steam: Place on rack and steam over boiling water for 15 minutes.

To bake, go to page 42 for baked bao dough recipe.

BUN DOUGH FOR BAKING

Bao

MAKES ABOUT 24

Some feel the baked filled buns are even more popular than the steamed ones. They usually have a shiny glaze and look very inviting. Fill them with your favorite filling, bake, and serve.

1 packet active dry yeast (2¼ teaspoons)
1¾ cup warm water
¾ cup sugar
1 teaspoon baking powder
6½ cups unsifted all-purpose flour
1 large egg, beaten
1 teaspoon water
1 teaspoon sugar
Red food coloring (optional)

In a standing mixer using a dough hook, dissolve yeast in warm water (105 to 110°F). Add sugar and mix. Add baking powder and flour and mix on low speed for 15 minutes. If you do not have a standing mixer, knead dough by hand on a floured board. Check if dough is smooth and elastic. If not, mix for 5 more minutes and check again. Dough should be smooth and elastic. Remove and place in a very large bowl as it will double in size. Cover with plastic wrap and then a clean kitchen towel and place in an unheated oven. Set 2 cups of boiling water to the side of the dough bowl to warm the oven slightly. Let double in size, 2 to 3 hours.

Punch down dough and place in mixer again with dough hook. Mix on low speed for 5 more minutes. Divide into 24 pieces and fill with about 1 tablespoon of sweet bean filling (page 91) or savory filling like Char Siu (page 124). The edges can be placed on the bottom so the top is round and smooth. Mix beaten egg with 1 teaspoon water and 1 teaspoon sugar. Brush bao with the egg, water, sugar wash for a shiny finish. If adding a red dot, dry bao for at least 15 minutes. Using a round chopstick, dip in red food coloring and place a dot in the center of the bao.

Bake at 350°F until done, about 20 minutes.

STEAMED PLAIN BREAD
Mantou

MAKES 8 ROLLS

Mantou will remind you of the tender outside of a Char Siu Bao. This is called a Chinese steamed bun and is not filled. Traditionally served in Northern China, it's now common throughout the Chinese diaspora. Loved for their tender, smooth texture from steaming, they can range in size from 1½ inches to much larger.

1 cup whole milk, substitute lower fat milk or soy or coconut milk
1 teaspoon active dry yeast
2½ tablespoons sugar
2¾ cups all-purpose flour

Combine milk, yeast, and sugar together in the bowl of a standing mixer. You do not need to first activate the yeast. Stir together using two chopsticks. Add the flour and on the lowest speed, combine ingredients for 1 minute using the dough hook attachment. Then increase the speed and let the machine knead the dough for 7 minutes. Remove and form into a log. Cut into 8 pieces. Place so pieces are not touching in an oiled steamer or on individually cut parchment papers and cook for 10 minutes. Best if eaten that day.

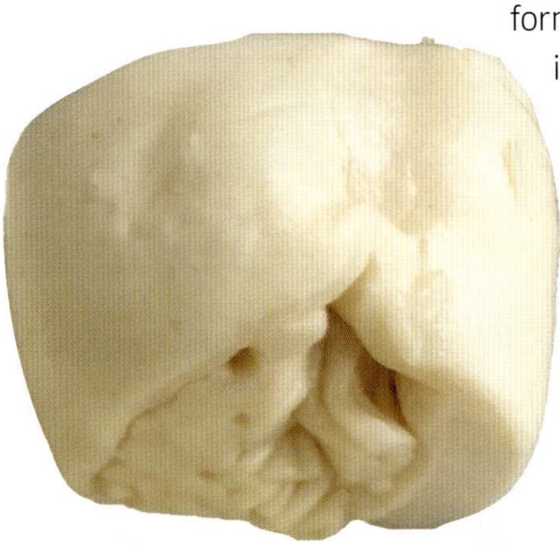

CHINESE SAUSAGE IN BUN

Lap Cheong Bao

MAKES 8

Chinese sausages are pork sausages with a sweet flavor. There are liver-versions, but those are less popular. If you have the time, use the baked Bao (page 42) or the steamed Bao (page 40) recipes for best results. However, when you are in a rush, the canned, refrigerated biscuits or rolls in the market are good substitutions.

8 Chinese sweet sausages (lap cheong)
1 (16.3-ounce) can refrigerated ready-to-bake original, flaky or Hawaiian Sweetbread rolls
1 tablespoon sugar
Optional: 1 large egg, beaten

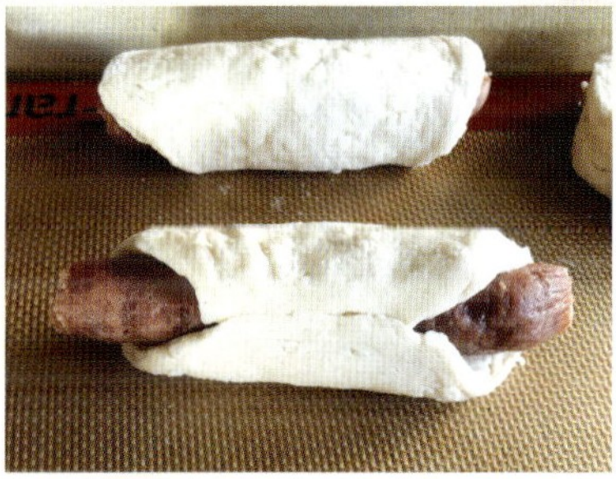

Put sausages in a sauce pan and cover with water on high heat. With a knife, puncture holes in the sausage casing. When water comes to a boil, reduce to medium heat and cook for 10 minutes to remove excess fat. Cool sausages and remove casing, if needed. You may not be able to remove the skins of sausage, depending on the brand.

Preheat oven to 350°F.

Using a rolling pin, flatten each biscuit and dust both sides with a sprinkle of sugar. Roll so that a sausage will stick out a bit on both ends and it is wide enough to seal the sausage around the middle. Depending on the size of your sausage, 4 × 3-inches should work. Place the sausage on the bread and seal in the middle. Place with the seam side down on a baking tray lined with parchment or foil. Repeat until all sausages are completed. Brush tops with the beaten egg. Bake until bread is cooked and tops are golden brown, about 15 minutes (refer to package directions). You may slice the Lap Cheong Bao in half or in smaller pieces as an appetizer.

Can be baked ahead and frozen. Reheat frozen baked bao by steaming or baking 325°F for 25 minutes in loosely wrapped foil. If defrosted, reduce the time to reheat.

Variation: Substitute any sausage for the lap cheong. Try chicken sausages, Andouille, Portuguese sausages, or hot dogs.

CHICKEN AND MUSHROOM BUNS

Doong Goo Gai Bao

MAKES 8 BUNS

Meat filled buns are a popular dim sum throughout China and this chicken-mushroom version is especially delightful. Garlic chives are also called Chinese chives and they are flat, instead of hollow as American chives are. They add an earthy, slightly garlicky flavor.

FILLING

- 1 pound dried black mushrooms, rehydrated, stemmed, caps chopped
- 2 tablespoons vegetable oil
- 1 tablespoon minced garlic
- 1 tablespoon minced fresh ginger
- Salt and freshly ground black pepper to taste
- 1 pound raw ground chicken
- ⅓ cup chopped garlic chives
- 1 teaspoon sesame oil

- ½ recipe Bao (Steamed Bun Dough, page 40)
- Oil to brush tops (optional)
- Red food coloring (optional)

Soak mushrooms in hot or boiling water for at least 30 minutes. Discard stems and chop the caps. Retain the flavorful liquid to add to soups or use it in place of water for any cooking. To make filling, heat skillet over high heat. Add the oil and swirl to coat the bottom of the pan. Add garlic and ginger to hot oil and stir-fry, stirring, until soft, about 2 minutes. Add chopped mushrooms and cook until soft, about 5 to 6 minutes. Season with salt and pepper and allow to cool.

Transfer mixture to medium bowl; add chicken, chives, and sesame oil; stir to blend. Chill for at least 30 minutes.

Prepare Bao according to directions. Divide the filling into 8 portions. Flatten the bao dough and place the filling in center of each circle of dough. Pull dough up and around filling; pinch edges together to seal. Keep pinched portion on top of bao for a "knot" on top or place pinched portion on bottom for a rounder look. Brush tops with vegetable oil, if round on top. Steam, seam side down, on parchment paper squares until the chicken filling is cooked, 15 to 20 minutes.

For round bao: If you would like to add a symbol to differentiate the types of bao, place the "seams" of the bao on the bottom instead of the top so you have a rounded, smooth top. Dot a round chopstick or straw in red food coloring and make 1, 2, or 3 dots on the top of the bao.

IMPORTANT SYMBOLS

Both baked and steamed bao are stamped with a red food coloring dot or other symbols to communicate what type of filling you are selecting. Royal Kitchen in Chinatown offers 11 types of baked bao. Liana Benn of the popular take-out restaurant says even the ones with distinct shapes need to be marked, such as the longer shaped Chinese sausage could get confused with the similarly-shaped Portuguese sausage bao or hot dog.

STEAMED PORK AND VEGETABLE BUNS

Choy Yuk Bao

MAKES ABOUT 16 BUNS

Bamboo shoots, carrots, and mushrooms are often used in vegetable fillings for buns, but here's a unique blend of won bok cabbage with mushrooms and pork, spiced with some hot pepper flakes.

FILLING

3 cups finely shredded won bok cabbage
1½ teaspoons salt
6 large dried black mushrooms, softened in hot water, stems discarded, minced
½ pound ground pork
¼ cup minced green onion
1 large egg, slightly beaten
2 tablespoons soy sauce
1 teaspoon sesame oil
½ teaspoon hot red chili pepper flakes (optional)
¼ teaspoon white pepper (optional)

1 recipe Bao (Steamed Bun Dough, page 40)

In large bowl, sprinkle cabbage with salt and let stand 20 to 25 minutes. Squeeze cabbage to remove water, then transfer to another bowl. Discard cabbage liquid.

Combine cabbage with remaining filling ingredients; toss to mix well and set aside. Cover and refrigerate for up to 1 day until ready to use.

Prepare Bao according to directions. Roll out Bao dough into a 16-inch log and slice into 16 portions. Roll or press each portion into a 3-inch circle. Place 2 tablespoons filling in center of each circle of dough. Gather dough around filling, stretching slightly, if necessary, to form pouch; twist to seal top.

Many recipes call for ground white pepper rather than black pepper. They are the same pepper, but vary from when they are picked and how they are processed. White pepper is less spicy, but is described as earthy and musty. In Chinese, Swedish, Vietnamese and French foods, it is often preferred over black pepper.

Place buns on 3-inch squares of parchment, sealed side up. Arrange 2 inches apart in steamer. Cover and let rise about 45 minutes. Cover and steam 10 to 15 minutes or until puffed and dry to the touch. Serve warm buns with desired sauce (page 170).

PAN-FRIED CHIVE AND SHRIMP BUNS

Gau Choy Har Bao

MAKES ABOUT 16 BUNS

You'll enjoy this shrimp filled bun because the texture is chewy and crispy from pan frying. The texture of the bun adds a new dimension to what would otherwise be an ordinary steamed bun.

FILLING

1 pound raw shrimp, peeled and deveined, rough chopped
2 cups chopped garlic chives
2 large eggs, beaten
1½ teaspoons toasted sesame oil
1 teaspoon finely chopped fresh ginger
Salt and freshly ground black pepper

Bao (Steamed Bun Dough, page 40)

2 tablespoons peanut, vegetable, or canola oil
2 cups chicken broth

To prepare filling, combine shrimp, chives, eggs, sesame oil, and ginger; season with salt and pepper to taste. (To taste, add salt and pepper then cook a small sample). Mix thoroughly. Divide into 16 portions.

Follow the Bao instructions on page 40; divide dough into 16 portions. Place filling with dough, pleat the edge of the wrappers to bring the top folds together, then pinch and twist them to seal. Place on individual 3 × 3-inch pieces of parchment. Repeat with remaining dough and filling. You may twist the bao closed with a top knot. Cover buns with a damp towel and allow them to rest, refrigerated, until puffed, about 1½ hours.

Heat a large skillet over medium heat. Add oil and swirl to coat bottom of pan. Add buns to hot oil, flat side down, and brown about 5 minutes. Add 1 cup chicken broth or water and cover the pan immediately to avoid spattering. Allow buns to steam until liquid evaporates completely and bottoms are crisp, about 10 minutes. Check after 5 minutes; if the stock has evaporated but the buns are not cooked, add more stock in ¼-cup increments. If the buns are done but stock remains in the pan, drain it and allow the bottoms to crisp. Serve immediately.

GREEN ONION CAKE
Chun Yau Bang

MAKES 8

Similar to a Mexican tortilla or Indian paratha; this unleavened bread is thin and chewy. Northern Chinese serve it instead of rice. In Western menus, it makes a delicious appetizer or snack. Using boiling water is the trick to get the desired texture of this popular bread.

1 cup all-purpose flour, not sifted
½ teaspoon salt
⅓ cup boiling water
4 strips bacon
2 stalks green onions, thinly chopped
About 3 tablespoons sesame seeds
1 tablespoon vegetable oil

In a bowl, combine flour and salt. Mix in boiling water with a pair of chopsticks until dough is evenly moistened and begins to hold together.

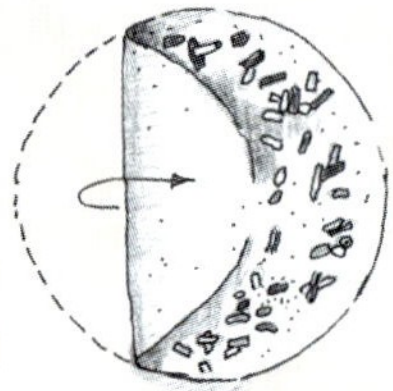

On a lightly floured board, knead dough until smooth and satiny, about 3 minutes. Cover dough and let rest at room temperature for at least 30 minutes.

Meanwhile, in a frying pan over medium heat, cook bacon until crisp; drain (reserve drippings) and crumble.

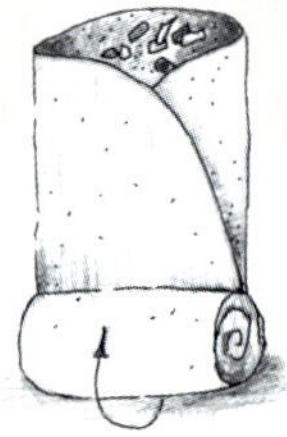

On a lightly floured board, divide dough into 8 pieces and roll out each piece into a flat, thin round. Brush each pancake with ½ teaspoon bacon drippings, then sprinkle bacon bits and green onions. Using your hands, fold over left and right side of the pancake, then roll the dough into a tube shape (see diagram), coil the tube into a stacked bun shape. Set aside and finish the other seven. Then flatten each bun gently with a rolling pin as thin as you can.

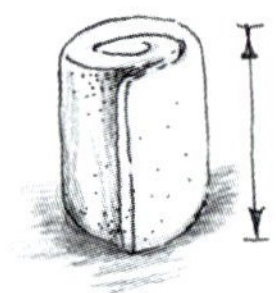

Sprinkle ½ teaspoon sesame seeds on each side of circle and lightly press into dough. At this point you can stack rounds (separate with sheets of parchment), cover, and chill for up to 8 hours.

This is an clever method for making sure the cakes are flaky. The coiling results in the beautiful layers.

In a wide frying pan, heat oil over medium-high heat. Cook cakes until golden brown (about 2 to 3 minutes on a side). Serve hot.

Variations:

- Add ½ teaspoon of crushed Sichuan peppercorns for a distinctive flavor.
- For a vegetarian version, omit bacon and brush with peanut, sesame, or vegetable oil.

MANDARIN PANCAKE
Bang

MAKES 4 TO 6 SERVINGS

These flatbreads were more common in the wheat-rich Northern China, rather than in the South. They are useful as a wrap for duck with a dab of plum or hoisin sauce and with strips of green onions and Chinese parsley. Even your children will have fun making these. Just be careful, because the boiling water is crucial to achieving the texture.

2 cups all-purpose flour
¾ cup boiling water
½ teaspoon toasted sesame oil
1 tablespoon toasted sesame oil for brushing

This recipe highlights a great technique to achieve very thin flat breads. Oiling the dough, putting two pieces together, and rolling them out. Cooking them, then separating them.

Mix flour with chopsticks, slowly pouring in boiling water and ½ teaspoon toasted sesame oil to form dough. Knead for about 10 minutes by hand or in a standing mixer with a dough hook attachment. Let stand for 30 minutes. Shape dough into long cylinder, cut to form golf ball-size pieces and flatten with palm into 2-inch diameter cakes.

Brush a light coat of sesame oil on one and pair with another pancake to form a sandwich with the oiled sides in. Use rolling pin and flatten to 8-inch diameter sandwiches.

Fry in flat, ungreased skillet over low heat until both sides turn slightly yellow. Remove from skillet and separate into two thin pancakes. Line steamer with cheesecloth and steam pancakes for 10 minutes before serving. Fold into quarters and cover with cloth until ready to serve. Serve hot or cold with any meat, but especially good with Roast Duck (page 142), Peking Duck (page 140), or Mu Shu Pork (page 122). Serve hot.

VARIATIONS

Make one or more of the fillings that follow. Arrange desired fillings into center of each pancake; roll like you would a jelly roll.

GREEN ONION WITH PORK FILLING

- ½ pound raw pork
- 2 tablespoons soy sauce
- 1 teaspoon Shaoxing wine, substitute dry sherry
- 1 teaspoon cornstarch
- 5 tablespoons oil
- 2 cups chopped green onion
- ½ teaspoon salt

Slice pork into strips. Mix pork with soy sauce, wine, and cornstarch. Heat oil and sauté pork until color changes. Add green onion and salt; mix well. Remove from heat before onion loses moisture. .

SAUTÉED SHRIMP FILLING

- 1 pound raw shrimp
- 1 teaspoon cornstarch
- 1 teaspoon Shaoxing wine, substitute dry sherry
- 3 tablespoons oil
- ½ teaspoon salt
- Dash of sugar

Shell, devein, and chop shrimp. Sprinkle with cornstarch and wine. Heat oil and sauté shrimp over high heat until color changes. Add salt and sugar; stir well.

Other fillings: scrambled eggs, thinly slivered fried potato, slivered char siu, sautéed bean sprouts.

SPRING ROLLS
Chun Guen

MAKES ABOUT 30

The crisp, crunchy texture of fried spring rolls and its flavorful filling makes this dish one of the most popular items of a meal or as an appetizer. Add Chinese raw fishcake, chopped shrimp, char siu, roast pork, or any of your favorite ingredients.

FILLING

¾ cup finely diced dried black mushroom (about 5 dried), rehydrated
½ pound boneless, skinless chicken, slivered
1 tablespoon Shaoxing wine or dry sherry
¼ teaspoon salt
1 teaspoon cornstarch
3 tablespoons vegetable oil
½ cup minced green onion
1½ cups slivered bamboo shoots
1½ cups bean sprouts
¼ teaspoon salt
2 tablespoons soy sauce

2 (6.75-ounce) packages spring roll wrappers
2 teaspoons cornstarch
2 tablespoons water, or use mushroom liquid
1 quart vegetable or canola oil for frying

Soak mushrooms in hot water for at least 30 minutes. Discard stems and finely dice caps. Mix chicken, wine, salt, and cornstarch; sauté in hot oil 1 minute. Add remaining filling ingredients; stir-fry an additional minute. Set aside to cool.

Divide filling into 30 portions. Place one filling portion on middle of spring roll wrapper. Moisten left and right edges of wrapper with mixture of cornstarch and water (or the mushroom liquid). Fold bottom edge up, left and right edges over, and roll. Moisten top edge with cornstarch-water mixture and seal.

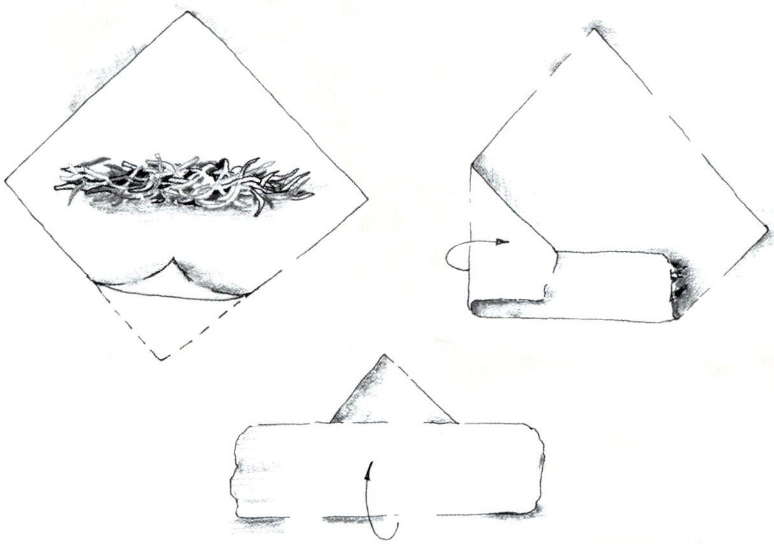

Deep fry in oil heated to 375°F until golden brown and crisp. Drain on cooling rack or paper towels.

Traditionally served with a Sweet-and-Sour Sauce (page 174) or choose your favorite sauce (page 170).

Variation: Substitute beef, pork, crab, or shrimp for chicken.

Note: Filled rolls may be frozen before frying.

Other Dim Sum

There are no hard and fast rules for what is considered dim sum. In addition to dumplings, diners would be disappointed with no simmered beef tripe (two types no less), sticky rice with sausage and mushrooms, taro puffs, or steamed, then pan-fried taro cake. One of the prettiest packages is the marinated chicken in parchment wrapping.

These delicacies are not classified as dumplings as they do not have a separate covering, but are "mandatory" at dim sum restaurants. Every dish offers a variety of different flavors and textures, which makes going to yum cha so pleasurable.

TURNIP PASTRY
Lo Bak Soo

MAKES 8 TO 12 PASTRIES

The name Lo Bak refers to the distinct taste of the long turnip. Soo means a flaky pastry. This is an updated version of a traditional recipe to meet today's busy lifestyle.

2½ cups shredded raw turnips
3 cups iced water
2 teaspoons salt, divided
1½ cups minced roast pork
⅓ cup small dried shrimp, soaked in water
¼ cup minced green onions
½ teaspoons sugar
1 (16.3-ounce) package refrigerated butter flake dinner rolls or crescents
1 large egg, beaten

Combine turnips, water, and 1½ teaspoons of salt in a large bowl; refrigerate 45 to 60 minutes. Rinse and drain turnips well; squeeze to remove as much liquid as possible. Grease baking sheet; set aside.

Mix turnips with pork, shrimp, green onions, sugar, and remaining ½ teaspoon salt. Separate rolls and roll each into 4-inch circle on lightly floured surface. Place ¼ cup turnip mixture in center of circle; pull dough up and around filling; pinch to seal seams. Place, seam side down, on prepared baking sheet.

Bake at 375°F for 10 minutes. Brush tops of rolls with beaten egg. Bake an additional 10 to 15 minutes or until golden. Serve immediately.

STUFFED EGGPLANT

Yeung Ai Gwa

MAKES 8 TO 10 SERVINGS

Cooked eggplant has a wonderful texture. Topped with a tasty filling, it is a much-ordered dish in the dim sum tea houses.

FILLING

- ½ pound ground pork
- ¼ cup raw Chinese fishcake, substitute minced raw shrimp
- 15 water chestnuts, minced
- 2 dried black mushrooms, soaked in hot water for 30 minutes
- 1 teaspoon oyster sauce
- 1 teaspoon salt
- 1 tablespoon minced green onions

- 1 pound long Asian eggplants, washed and patted dry
- Salt
- ⅓ cup flour
- 3 tablespoons cornstarch
- 1 large egg, slightly beaten
- 1 quart vegetable or canola oil for frying

SAUCE

- ½ cup chicken broth or water
- 1 teaspoon soy sauce
- 1 teaspoon sugar
- ¼ teaspoon salt
- 1 teaspoon cornstarch
- 1 tablespoon water

Mix filling ingredients well and set aside.

Cut off ends diagonally from eggplants; discard. Cut eggplants diagonally into 1-inch lengths, making 14 to 16 total pieces. Cut out ¼-inch wide wedge two-thirds of the way through from the side of each piece to make room for the stuffing; lightly salt and let stand 20 minutes.

Wipe with paper towels to remove salt and moisture. Stuff cavity of each eggplant with about 2 teaspoons of filling mixture.

Combine flour and cornstarch in bowl. Dip stuffed eggplant pieces into egg then into flour mixture, shaking off any excess flour.

Deep fry in oil heated to 365°F until golden brown on all sides. Drain on absorbent paper. Place on serving dish.

To prepare the sauce, combine chicken broth or water, soy sauce, sugar, and salt in small saucepan; bring to a boil. Dissolve cornstarch in 1 tablespoon water; stir into sauce and cook 30 seconds or until sauce is thickened. Drizzle sauce over eggplants to serve. Serve with a dipping sauce of your choice (page 170).

Note: Round eggplants may be substituted; cut eggplants into ½-inch rounds then cut into semicircles to make about 14 pieces. Spread pork/fishcake mixture on top of each eggplant slice; proceed as above.

Variation: Wash and seed 1 pound bell peppers of any color. Cut into wedges, stuff with filling and fry as instructed.

LEAF TRIPE
Ngau Jup

MAKES ABOUT 3 TO 4 DIM SUM-SIZED SERVINGS

This white tripe is called leaf or book tripe as it resembles the pages you turn in a book. This preparation is popular as it is a form of Hawaiian-style poke, usually seafood flavored in a spicy sauce and eaten as a perfect pūpū (appetizer).

10 cups boiling water
1½ inches ginger, peeled or not peeled, cut into slices
1 pound leaf tripe
1-inch ginger, peeled, cut into fine matchsticks, for garnish
3 tablespoons green onions, cut in long strips as garnish
1½ tablespoon soy sauce
1 teaspoon toasted sesame oil
¼ teaspoon chili oil, substitute hot sauce or chili peppers of your choice

Heat water with ginger slices, when boiling, add large pieces of leaf tripe and cook on high for 20 minutes. Test. If it is the texture you like, cool in ice water bath. If you want it more tender, cook longer. Check every few minutes. Discard boiled ginger slices. Slice tripe to desired shape. Garnish with julienned ginger, green onion strips, soy sauce, sesame oil, and chili oil. Serve at room temperature or chilled. This recipe is easily made the day before and refrigerated.

HONEYCOMB TRIPE

Ngau Bak Yip

MAKES ABOUT 4 SERVINGS

This part of the beef tripe is named for the crisscross patterns like a honeycomb from a bee's nest. Long cooking makes this offal tender, flavorful and sought after on a dim sum menu.

1½ inches ginger, peeled or not peeled, cut into slices
1 pound honeycomb tripe
1 tablespoon peanut, vegetable, or canola oil
6 star anise
2 cups water
½ cup soy sauce
2 inches ginger, peeled and sliced into matchsticks, for garnish
2 tablespoons broken Chinese slab sugar, substitute brown sugar
1 tablespoon Shaoxing wine, substitute dry sherry
1 teaspoon toasted sesame oil
1 teaspoon white pepper
1 tablespoon cornstarch mixed with 2 tablespoons water (optional)
3 stalks green onion for garnish

Boil 10 cups of water in a pot and add first batch of ginger slices. Trim fat from tripe. When boiling, add tripe and cook for 20 minutes. Cut in half or quarters if it does not fit the pot. Cool tripe in ice water bath then drain in a colander. Discard these cooked ginger slices. In a large sauce pan or Dutch oven, heat oil on high heat and cook half of the ginger slices and star anise until brown, about 5 minutes. Add drained tripe and cook for 5 minutes. Add 2 cups water, soy sauce, ginger matchsticks, sugar, Shaoxing wine, sesame oil, and white pepper; bring to a boil. Reduce to simmer and cook for 1 hour uncovered. Check tripe texture. If the texture is tender, serve as is or if you prefer a thicker gravy, add cornstarch mixture. Add to sauce and stir until thickened. Garnish with green onions. No sauce is needed, but you could make a dipping sauce of your choice (page 170).

STUFFED TOFU

Yeung Dow Foo

MAKES ABOUT 10 PIECES

Stuffed Tofu is a popular dish in restaurants and at home. Usually steamed and served with a simple gravy, it could also be deep-fried for a different texture. You can substitute your favorite stuffing.

1 (21-ounce) block firm tofu, drained at least an hour
1 pound minced raw shrimp, or half shrimp and half raw Chinese fishcake
¼ pound ground pork
4 ounces (half can) water chestnuts, chopped
2 stalks green onions minced
2 teaspoons oyster sauce
1 teaspoon salt
½ teaspoon white pepper
1 teaspoon cornstarch
¼ cup chicken broth
1 tablespoon oyster sauce

Oil to grease the pans

Chopped green onions and Chinese parsley leaves for garnish

Place tofu on a plate and weigh it down with another plate on top and a heavy can on top of the plate. Drain water repeatedly, then cut tofu into 10 equal triangle shapes and place on paper towels to continue draining. In a bowl, mix shrimp, pork, water chestnuts, green onions, salt, and white pepper. Using a knife, cut the long side of the tofu triangle, being careful not to cut all the way through. This makes a pocket for the filling. Carefully fill the tofu pockets with the shrimp-pork filling. The filling can overflow from the tofu. Place stuffed tofu with the filling facing up or place on side on an oiled parchment-lined pan and place in steamer. Cook until filling is cooked, about 15 minutes. In a saucepan, mix cornstarch with chicken broth and oyster sauce. Cook on medium high until gravy has thickened, about 3 minutes. Place cooked tofu on a serving platter. Pour gravy over tofu, garnish, and serve hot or at room temperature.

Variation: Add one minced black mushroom cap to filling after soaking it in hot water. Serve on a bed of blanched soft greens such as spinach, bok choy, or baby bok choy.

Stuffed tofu in this style is called Hakka-style tofu. The Hakka people are called the nomads of China. Originally from Northern China, they moved to Southern China and were known as hard workers. The women never bound their feet, so were able to work the fields.

STEAMED BEEF MEATBALLS
Jing Ngau Yuk Yuen

MAKES 4 TO 6 SERVINGS

These tender meatballs are soft and flavorful. When served at a dim sum restaurant, they are always steamed. Showing the influence of British rule in Hong Kong, these meatballs are often served with a side dip of Worcestershire sauce.

- 1 pound lean ground beef
- 2 tablespoons finely chopped water chestnuts
- 2 tablespoons finely chopped onions
- 2 tablespoons chopped rehydrated black mushrooms, stems discarded
- 1 large clove garlic, finely chopped
- 1/4 cup chopped green onions
- 1 large egg white
- 1 tablespoon soy sauce
- 1 tablespoon toasted sesame oil
- 1 tablespoon cornstarch
- 1/2 teaspoon salt
- 1/2 teaspoon white pepper
- 1/2 teaspoon sugar
- Chopped green onions or Chinese parsley leaves for garnish

Combine ingredients except garnishes in a large mixing bowl and mix thoroughly using a pair of chopsticks. Then mix by hand stirring only in one direction. Shape into 2-inch meatballs. Place 2 or 3 on a small plate and steam on high until meatball is cooked, about 20 minutes. Garnish with chopped green onions or Chinese parsley leaves. Serve with dipping sauce of Worcestershire sauce or a dip of your choice (page 170).

EASY CURRIED CHICKEN TURNOVERS

Ga Lei Gok

MAKES ABOUT 8 TO 10 TURNOVERS

These spicy, curried turnovers are a refreshing change of flavor and they are especially tasty when served hot. This recipe is an easy-to-make version of the traditional turnovers to fit today's busy lifestyle as it uses store-bought refrigerated dough.

FILLING

1 medium dried black mushroom, soaked in hot water 30 minutes

⅔ cup chopped boneless, skinless chicken breasts or thighs

4 medium raw shrimp, cleaned and minced

1 teaspoon vegetable oil

2 water chestnuts, minced

1 large cloud ear fungus, rehydrated, minced

1 tablespoon minced Chinese parsley or green onion

SEASONINGS

1 teaspoon soy sauce

¼ teaspoon sugar

¼ teaspoon curry powder

¼ teaspoon salt

1 (16.3-ounce) tube refrigerated flaky biscuits or crescents

1 large egg, beaten

Discard mushroom stems. Mince rehydrated mushrooms and set aside. Stir-fry chicken and shrimp in hot oil for 30 seconds. Add all remaining ingredients except biscuits. Stir-fry additional minute. Set aside and cool slightly. Separate into 8 portions.

(left) dried cloud ear fungus
(right) rehydrated cloud ear fungus

Flatten each biscuit to make a 3-inch circle. Place 1 tablespoon curried chicken filling in the center of each circle; fold dough over to make half-moon; pinch edges to seal. Place on ungreased cookie sheet. Brush tops with beaten egg mixture. Bake at 400°F for 10 to 12 minutes or until golden brown.

Variations: Ground pork may be substituted for chicken.

PAPER-WRAPPED CHICKEN

Ji Bao Gai

MAKES ABOUT 30 PACKAGES

Good food comes in small packages when you wrap it the Chinese way. You place morsels of marinated chicken, seafood, or meat on cooking parchment squares, fold them into tiny envelopes, and cook the packets immediately before serving. To eat, you open the wrapping with your fingers and pick up each bite with chopsticks or a fork. This is also called gift-wrapped chicken. It is found more often in San Francisco, rather than Hawai'i. However, since it is so delicious, more Hawai'i restaurants are offering what is presented like a present.

- 1 tablespoon soy sauce
- 1 tablespoon Shaoxing wine or dry sherry
- 1 tablespoon hoisin sauce
- 1 teaspoon cornstarch
- 1 teaspoon vegetable oil
- ½ teaspoon toasted sesame oil
- ½ teaspoon sugar
- ½ teaspoon minced fresh ginger
- Dash of white pepper
- 1 pound chicken breasts, skinned, boned, and cut in bite-size pieces
- 2 ounces Virginia ham, sandwich ham, or Chinese sausages
- 5 stalks green onions
- 30 Chinese parsley leaves
- Vegetable oil to fill your frying pan to 1½-inch depth

In a bowl, combine soy sauce, wine, hoisin sauce, cornstarch, vegetable oil, sesame oil, sugar, ginger, and pepper. Add chicken and marinate for 30 minutes.

Cut ham, if used, in matchstick pieces. If you use Chinese sausages, steam them on a rack over boiling water for 15 minutes, then cut diagonally in slices ⅛-inch thick; you should have 30 slices.

Cut green onions in 1½-inch lengths, then slice lengthwise in thin shreds.

Cut cooking parchment into 30 (5-inch) squares. Substitute foil.

To wrap chicken: In center of each parchment square, place 1 piece chicken, 3 strips ham (or 1 slice Chinese sausage), several shreds of green onion, and a Chinese parsley leaf. Turn one corner up over filling. Fold adjacent corners in toward center, overlapping and enclosing filling. Fold filled part of packet in half (see dotted line). Slide fourth corner all the way down into space between layers of paper to seal each packet. At this point you can cover and refrigerate up to 6 hours until ready to cook.

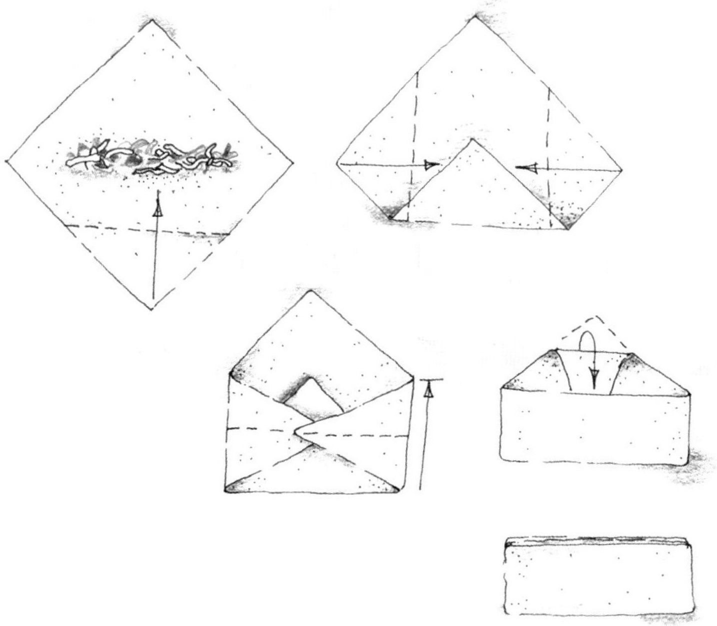

In a deep pan that is at least 6 inches in diameter, pour vegetable oil to a depth of $1\frac{1}{2}$ inches and heat to 350°F on a deep-frying thermometer. Fry 4 to 6 packets at a time, turning occasionally, for 3 minutes or until chicken is cooked. Remove with a slotted spoon and drain on paper towels. Keep warm in a 200°F oven until all are cooked. Serve hot and let your guests unwrap the "present."

Or, to bake instead of fry, arrange packets in a single layer in a shallow, rimmed baking pan. Bake in a 400°F oven for 12 minutes.

TARO PUFFS
Woo Gok

MAKES 10

These fried yet light puffs of seasoned mashed taro surround a tasty meat and vegetable filling. The restaurants are able to create those wispy shreds of fried honeycomb-like goodness by using lard in the covering and frying at a high heat. At home it is not always easy to recreate that technique. A good solution is to do a traditional flour, egg wash and then panko bread crumb coating. The same appealing crunch is achieved.

1 pound taro root, Chinese land taro preferred

FILLING

1 tablespoon vegetable oil
1 cup ground pork or diced roast pork (siu jee yuk)
3 dried black mushrooms, soaked in hot water for 30 minutes
¼ cup chopped green onions
2 tablespoons oyster sauce
¼ cup dried shrimp, soaked in water and minced
2 tablespoons toasted sesame oil
1 teaspoon Chinese Five Spice powder
1 tablespoon Shaoxing wine, substitute dry sherry
½ teaspoon salt
¼ teaspoon white pepper
¼ cup chicken broth
1 tablespoon cornstarch

COATING

2 tablespoons cornstarch
½ cup chicken broth
1 tablespoon oil or shortening
½ teaspoon salt
½ cup flour
1 large egg, beaten
2 cups dry bread crumbs or panko
4 cups peanut, vegetable, or canola oil

Peel taro and cut into ½-inch slices. Place in a steamer and cook on high heat until very tender, about 1 hour. Set aside. Heat a wok or skillet and add 1 tablespoon oil. On medium high heat, stir-fry pork until cooked, about 3 minutes, add mushrooms, onions, oyster sauce, minced shrimp, sesame oil, Chinese Five Spice, wine, salt, and white pepper. Cook for 4 minutes. Mix broth with cornstarch until dissolved. Bring to a boil and stir until sauce is thickened, about 3 minutes. Remove from heat, cool, then refrigerate.

Mix 2 tablespoons cornstarch with ½ cup broth in a sauce pan and heat over high heat. Bring to a boil; cool. In a large bowl, mash taro and add 1 tablespoon oil and salt. Gradually add the cornstarch mixture. You may not need to add all of it. It should resemble thick mashed potatoes. Divide the taro mixture into 10. Take one and form a ball and flatten to ½-inch high. If needed, use cornstarch to keep the mixture from sticking to your hands. Place 1 tablespoon of the filling in the taro and then close, forming an oval shape. Roll in flour, dip in the beaten egg and roll in bread crumbs or panko. Heat oil until 350°F and fry until golden brown, about 4 minutes. Drain and serve.

STEAMED TARO CAKE
Woo Tau Go

MAKES TWO 9-INCH CAKES

This dish nearly made the Hawai'i's Top 10 list because of Hawai'i residents' love of taro. It is filled with savory bits of meat and umami-loaded mushrooms and salted turnip (chung choy) and topped with green onions or Chinese olives (larm see or larm gok). The texture is dense, not light. It can be eaten after steamed, but some enjoy the crispy edges after being pan-fried with a bit of oil.

¼ pound roast pork (siu jee yuk) or char siu, chopped
2 Chinese sausages (lap cheong), diced
1 salted turnip (chung choy), soaked and diced
¼ cup dried shrimp, soaked in water and chopped
1 tablespoon oyster sauce
¾ teaspoon sugar
¾ teaspoon salt
½ teaspoon soy sauce
½ teaspoon Shaoxing wine, substitute dry sherry
½ teaspoon toasted sesame oil
1 pound taro, peeled and diced
½ cup chicken broth
2 cups Swans Down cake flour, substitute other cake flour
1½ cups chicken broth
2 tablespoons oil
¼ cup chopped green onions
4 Chinese olives (larm see), chopped for garnish
Sesame seeds for garnish (optional)

In a wok or skillet, stir-fry pork, lap cheong, chung choy, and shrimp with oyster sauce, sugar, salt, soy sauce, and wine and cook for 5 minutes. Add sesame oil and set aside in a bowl. Wash wok and heat taro with chicken broth. Bring to a boil, then reduce heat to medium high and cook until taro is tender, about 15 minutes. Do not undercook. Remove from heat.

In large bowl, combine cake flour and chicken broth until smooth. Oil two 9-inch cake pans. Divide the taro mixture into two parts and place evenly in pans. Cover with the cake mixture. Top with the meat mixture. Steam until mixture is cooked, about 30 minutes. Garnish with green onions and olives. Sprinkle sesame seeds, if adding. Cake should cool before slicing into traditional diamond shaped pieces. Pan fry in oil if you want to reheat or if you like it pan-fried.

Note: For the traditional dim sum texture, use Chinese dry land taro. Hawaiian, Samoan, and Japanese taros are heavier and wetter.

STICKY RICE WITH SAUSAGE AND MUSHROOMS

Ho Ip Fan

MAKES 8

One of the most popular dishes in Hawai'i is called Sticky Rice. Grains of glutinous rice, also called mochi rice, No Mai Fan, or sweet rice, are steamed with flavorful seasoned pork (char siu), dried shrimp, Chinese sausage, and umami-rich black mushrooms to create a winning dish.

Any combination of ingredients will result in a wonderful dish. Use chicken thighs, roast pork, or duck instead of the sweet barbecued pork (char siu) for a different flavor. Add a rich salted duck egg yolk and peanuts or black-eyed peas to mimic the popular Chinese tamale (joong).

- 2 Chinese sausages (lap cheong)
- 4 dried black mushrooms, soaked in hot water for 30 minutes
- 2 rice-cooker cups (1½ cups standard measuring cups) raw glutinous rice, rinsed and drained
- ½ teaspoon salt
- 4 cups chicken broth
- 2 teaspoons vegetable oil
- ½ cup chopped char siu
- 10 dried shrimp, soaked and chopped
- 2 tablespoons oyster sauce
- ½ teaspoon Chinese Five Spice powder
- ½ teaspoon sugar
- ¼ cup chopped green onions
- ¼ cup chopped Chinese parsley
- Dried lotus leaves, substitute banana leaves or ti leaves

Place sausages in a sauce pan and cover with water. Boil for 5 minutes to remove some of the oil. Depending on the brand of sausage, you may choose to discard the casing. Chop sausages and set aside.

Discard mushroom stems. Chop mushroom caps and set aside. In a sauce pan, place rice, salt, and enough chicken broth to measure ½-inch above the rice. Add water if needed. On medium heat, cook rice until tender and water has evaporated, about 30 minutes. Alternatively, cook in a rice cooker.

In a wok or a skillet, heat oil and stir-fry chopped sausage, char siu, mushrooms, and shrimp with oyster sauce, five spice powder, and sugar until mushrooms are tender, about 5 minutes. Mix with cooked rice and add green onions and Chinese parsley.

Soak lotus leaves in warm water for 30 minutes and cut in half. If using banana leaves, clean them. For ti leaves, remove stem, clean. Place about ½ cup of rice mixture in center and fold over into a packet in any shape. Many people like a rectangular shape. Tie with kitchen string. Repeat. Place in a steamer and cook for 10 to 15 minutes. Cut and discard string and serve in leaf. (The leaf is not to be eaten).

Variation: Roast pork or chicken thighs can be substituted for the char siu.

SAVORY TI LEAF WRAPPED DUMPLINGS
Ip Jai

MAKES ABOUT 30

These white morsels of sticky glutinous rice flour dough are beautifully wrapped in oiled ti leaves. They are filled with either a sweet mixture or savory morsels. This recipe is for salty tidbits of char siu and shrimp and vegetables. The sweet version of Ip Jai is on page 97.

DOUGH

4 cups glutinous rice flour (no mai fan, also called mochiko flour)
1½ cups water
1 tablespoon vegetable oil
1 teaspoon salt

FILLING

8 dried black mushrooms, soaked in hot water 30 minutes, retain liquid
1 tablespoon vegetable oil
1 pound char siu (sweet barbecue pork), chopped
¼ pound baked or sandwich ham, chopped
1 teaspoon salt
Pepper to taste
2 teaspoons brown sugar
2 cups shredded won bok cabbage
1 teaspoon soy sauce
1 tablespoon oyster sauce
1 pound shrimp, peeled, deveined and chopped
2 stalks green onion, finely chopped
1 teaspoon sesame oil

30 ti leaves for wrapping*
Additional vegetable oil for coating leaves
Optional red food coloring

Mix dough ingredients in a standing mixer until blended, about 3 minutes. Set aside.

Discard mushroom stems and dice mushrooms. In a large saucepan, add vegetable oil on medium high heat and add char siu, ham, salt, pepper, brown sugar, cabbage, mushrooms, soy sauce, oyster sauce and cook until cabbage is tender. Add the mushroom liquid if needed. Turn off heat and add shrimp, green onions, and sesame oil. Set aside.

Cut and wash 30 ti leaves. Remove the stem with a knife. Cut leaves into 3 × 7-inch strips. Soak in hot water to soften. Drain and pat dry. You may substitute foil strips, but the dish will not be as attractive. Oil generously on both sides.

Kristie Ou remembers her grandmother in China making both sweet and savory ip jai for the family. No red dots indicated what filling you would find inside. "It was a guessing game," she said, as she preferred the sweet filling.

Divide dough into 30 pieces. Shape each piece into a circle and flatten to 1/4-inch thick. Make a small dent in the center. Place 1 tablespoon of the filling in the center and press the edges together to seal. Place this filled dumpling on one end of the ti leaf and roll it. Fold and cover the bottom end of the dumpling, leaving the top of the dumpling open. Place in oiled steamer or place on individual squares of parchment and steam on high for 25 to 30 minutes. To distinguish it from the sweet variety, you may want to dip a rounded chopstick in food coloring and make a single dot in the center of the top.

*You may be able to put 2 to 4 ip jai in each ti leaf, depending on the size of the leaf. However, to make sure you have enough, prepare 30 leaves.

STUFFED MUSHROOM SIU MAI

Doong Goo Siu Mai

MAKES 18

Black mushrooms, called shiitake by the Japanese, are a beloved ingredient in all Chinese cooking. The tasty caps are stuffed with a tasty pork mixture and steamed until the mushrooms and filling are cooked.

18 dried Chinese black mushrooms

FILLING

¼ pound ground pork, substitute minced raw shrimp or raw Chinese fishcake
2 tablespoons minced green onion
2 tablespoons oyster sauce
1 teaspoon Shaoxing wine or dry sherry
1 teaspoon soy sauce
½ teaspoon cornstarch
¼ teaspoon salt

Chopped green onion or Chinese parsley leaf for garnish (optional)

Soak mushrooms in hot water for 1 hour or overnight in cold water in the refrigerator. Discard stems, but retain soaking liquid. Place mushrooms with liquid in a small sauce pan and heat on medium heat for 10 minutes to soften mushrooms. Combine remaining filling ingredients in small bowl; mix well and divide into 18 portions. Fill each mushroom with pork mixture; arrange in oiled pan or heat resistant plate and steam over boiling water until mushrooms are tender and filling is cooked; 10 to 12 minutes. Garnish and serve hot or at room temperature. These are tasty without a sauce, but if you prefer more spice, serve with a dipping sauce (page 170).

PEARL BALLS
Jing Ju Gee Yuk Yuen Zi

MAKES ABOUT 20 BALLS

This interesting looking dish is a standard in Hong Kong. A ball of seasoned ground pork surrounded by cooked grains of rice makes this steamed morsel look like a cute porcupine. Dim Sum and its many small bites are perfect for an appetizer party.

¾ cup raw short grain rice, substitute glutinous rice
1 cup cold water
1 pound ground pork
1 large egg, slightly beaten
1 tablespoon soy sauce
1½ teaspoons salt
½ teaspoon sugar
4 dried black mushrooms, soaked in hot water for 30 minutes
1 teaspoon minced fresh ginger
6 water chestnuts*, minced
¼ cup minced green onion

Soak rice in water for 2 hours; drain through a sieve and spread on cloth towel to dry.

Discard mushroom stems and mince caps. Combine pork, egg, soy sauce, salt, and sugar in mixing bowl; blend thoroughly. Add mushrooms, ginger, water chestnuts, and green onion; mix well and form 2 tablespoons of pork mixture into balls. Roll pork balls in the rice, pressing down gently but firmly so rice adheres to meat. Arrange pork balls on heat-proof plate; steam 30 minutes. Serve hot.

* Jicama or choy suey yam is always a substitute for water chestnuts.

SEASONED PEANUTS
Fa Sung

MAKES ABOUT 4 SERVINGS

Many are surprised to learn peanuts were easily grown in southern China. These delicious morsels are served at dim sum restaurants under chicken feet or meats, such as char siu or roast duck. The texture is crunchy or tender, depending how long you cook this legume. Red hulls left on are more attractive than just white, hulled nuts.

2-inch cinnamon stick
1 teaspoon Sichuan peppercorns
2 star anise
1 black cardamom
2 bay leaves
1 dried red chili pepper
1¾ cup raw peanuts, shelled, preferred with red skin (hull) still on
3 cups water
3 tablespoons soy sauce
1 tablespoon Chinese slab sugar, substitute brown sugar
1 teaspoon Chinese Five Spice powder

Cut cheesecloth into a 6-inch square. Place cinnamon, peppercorns, star anise, cardamom, bay leaves, and chili pepper inside cheesecloth. Bundle it and tie it with kitchen string. This makes the spices easier to remove later. Soak shelled peanuts in remaining ingredients with the spice bag for 2 hours. Bring to a boil, reduce heat to medium and cook for 20 minutes. Check if desired softness has been achieved. Cook longer if needed. Turn off heat. Cover and let sit in liquid for at least 1 hour. Drain. Keeps refrigerated up to 2 days.

Sweets

Back in the day, classic palate pleasers at the end of a Chinese meal would be platters of fruit in season—slices of melon, lychee, loquat, or longan. Chinese appreciate fruits of any kind. At Chinese New Year, stacked platters of oranges, tangerines, or kumquats are offered at every table.

Southern China was without cows, and therefore, little cream or butter. The Chinese menu, which offers numerous savory dishes, usually offers few simple desserts. However, in more recent years, Chinese have adapted recipes learned from others, such as the Portuguese in Macao, and made it their own. This chapter offers some delicious ways to conclude a Chinese meal. Elaborate desserts are usually presented at banquets.

NINE LAYER PUDDING
Gau Cang Go

MAKES ONE 9-INCH ROUND PUDDING

As children, we would fight over these soft pudding-like layers that would peel off one by one and be gobbled up. Fewer restaurants offer these as it takes time to steam each layer.

8 WHITE LAYERS

$2\frac{1}{2}$ cups sugar
$2\frac{1}{2}$ cups water
$2\frac{1}{2}$ cups tapioca starch, do not sift
2 tablespoons vegetable oil

TOP LAYER

$\frac{1}{4}$ cup Chinese slab sugar, broken, substitute dark brown sugar
$\frac{1}{4}$ cup water
$\frac{1}{4}$ cup tapioca starch, do not sift
2 teaspoons vegetable oil
2 tablespoons toasted white sesame seeds

Vegetable oil for greasing pan and layers

You can prepare the white layers and top layer ingredients concurrently, but use separate pots. Begin by boiling water and sugar. Let stand to cool. When cool, combine tapioca starch with sugar liquid in a mixing bowl and mix until smooth. Add oil and mix again.

Start water boiling in a wok or pot. Use vegetable oil to grease a 9-inch round cake pan. Pour in about $\frac{1}{3}$ cup of the white liquid to fill the pan and steam 5 minutes. Remove from steamer and lightly brush oil on top of layer. Wrap a clean dish towel around the lid to absorb liquid that may drop on pudding. Repeat steps to form 8 layers. For the final layer, pour the liquid that is colored brown from the Chinese slab sugar. Again, steam 5 minutes. Remove from steamer and set on a cooling rack. Brush with oil. Sprinkle sesame seeds and let cool for 24 hours. Invert the pudding using parchment paper to remove it from the pan. Cut into diamond shapes.

Why nine layers? Numbers 2, 8, and 9 are lucky numbers in the Chinese culture. Pagodas have nine stories. Dragons have nine likenesses or characteristics. Will we ever know the real reason?

BLACK SESAME PUDDING

Gee Ma Woo

MAKES ABOUT 4 SERVINGS

This warm soup or pudding is very satisfying with its sweet taste and attractive color. It makes a wonderful dessert.

2 cups long or medium grain white rice
2 cups black sesame seeds
4 cups cold water
1 cup Chinese slab sugar, broken, substitute dark brown sugar, plus more to taste
4 cups hot water, plus more to your preference

Wash rice and sesame seeds with water. Drain. Soak rice and sesame seeds in 4 cups water overnight. Put rice, sesame seeds, and the water in a food processor or blender and process until smooth. Put in a large pot and add 4 cups hot water. Bring to a boil and add additional hot water until it reaches the thickness you like. Add Chinese slab sugar and taste. Add additional sugar if you like it sweeter. Reduce temperature to low and cook for 20 minutes. Serve hot or at room temperature.

EASY NEW YEAR'S PUDDING

Nien Go

MAKES ONE 8-INCH PUDDING

This is quick and easy, yet still delicious. This version of the good luck pudding dessert served at the Chinese lunar new year is a baked version, instead of steamed.

- **1 (16-ounce) can yams, reserve liquid**
- **1 (16-ounce) box dark brown sugar**
- **1/3 cup grated coconut, sweetened or unsweetened**
- **2 tablespoons vegetable oil**
- **1/2 cup water**
- **20 ounces (about 5 1/4 cups) glutinous rice flour***
- **1 dried red date (hung jo)**
- **1 teaspoon sesame seeds**

Mash yams. Add brown sugar and coconut; stir until well-blended. Add oil, water, liquid from canned yams, and flour; mix well.

Pour batter into lightly greased 8-inch round cake pan (or line with ti leaves). Cover tightly with foil. Bake at 350°F for 2 hours. Alternatively, steam over boiling water for 2 hours. Cool; slice with plastic knife or dental floss. While pudding is still hot, place red date in center and sprinkle sesame seeds.

This is a dish for good luck. The sticky rice flour symbolizes a family who stays together. Red date is a dried jujube. Red is the favorite color of Chinese people. The sprinkling of sesame seeds symbolizes fertility; wishing your family many children.

*Glutinous or sweet rice flour, also called mochiko, is usually sold in 16-ounce bags or boxes. If you have leftover, store in freezer. It makes a great gluten-free thickener for gravy.

EASY SWEET BEAN PASTRY

Dow Sa Gok

MAKES ABOUT 12

An easy way to make your own sweet bean pastry dessert with refrigerated or frozen pie crusts. You'll enjoy it with a cup of tea.

1 (two 9-inch size) pie crusts, defrosted, if frozen
1 (about 18-ounce) can sweetened black or red bean paste*
1 large egg yolk, beaten
2 tablespoons water

Roll pie crust dough out on a floured surface to form 12 × 16-inch rectangle; cut into twelve 4-inch squares.

Divide bean paste into 12 portions and form each portion into a 2 × 2½-inch rectangle; place a piece in each pastry square. Fold two opposite ends of pastry over filling, then lap remaining sides over top to encase bean paste.

Place, seam side down, on baking pan sprayed with oil or lined with parchment; flatten each slightly with hand.

Mix egg yolk with water and brush on each pastry. Bake at 375°F for 45 minutes or until golden brown.

Cool on wire racks. Eat warm or at room temperature.

*Asian stores carry several kinds of canned sweetened bean pastes. Black or yellow bean pastes may be substituted for red bean paste. You could bake sweet potatoes of any variety, mash and sweeten with sugar, brown sugar, agave, or maple syrup and use in this recipe. Or make your own filling (page 91).

SWEET BEAN BUNS

Dow Sa Bao

MAKES ABOUT 24 BUNS

The soft, pillowy milk bread that surrounds char siu can also be a great combination with sweetened bean paste. Make your own with red beans or sweet potatoes and have a welcomed not-so-sweet dessert.

1 recipe for steamed buns (Bao) on page 40

1 recipe Sweet Bean Filling (dow sa; on next page) or buy 1½ cups store-bought sweetened red, black, or yellow bean paste

Follow instructions for Bao and use 1 tablespoon of the sweetened bean paste for each bao. Steam for 15 to 20 minutes and enjoy.

SWEET BEAN FILLING

½ pound dried red beans, substitute Japanese adzuki beans
1½ cups sugar
¼ teaspoon salt
1½ tablespoons peanut, vegetable, or canola oil

Wash and pick over beans, discarding any discolored ones and pebbles. Cover with at least 3 inches of tap water and soak overnight. The next day, drain water and rinse repeatedly until water is clear.

Put soaked beans in a large pot and cover with 3 inches of water. Bring to a boil on high, then reduce to low heat and cover. Cook until beans are soft, about 1½ hours. Cool, then mash beans and liquid by hand or use a food processor. Push through a strainer to remove skins. Add water through strainer to capture all bean mash. Discard skins.

Strain through a cheesecloth or clean kitchen cloth to remove almost all the water from the mixture. Repeat as needed so you have a dry bean mash. Add sugar, salt, and oil; mix thoroughly. Taste and additional sugar, if desired.

Place in a baking dish or casserole and cover with foil. Bake at 300°F for 10 minutes. Then reduce heat to 200°F for 1 hour. Beans will darken. This bean paste is ready to use in Dow Sa Bao or as a filling for Ip Jai (page 97), Chinese Doughnuts (page 94), or as a filling for Steamed Sponge Cake (page 100).

MANGO PUDDING

Mong Gwo Bou Din

MAKES 6 TO 8 SERVINGS

This delicious pudding is easy to make and is elegantly presented when poured into a fish mold or floral gelatin mold to set. To serve as a dinner dessert, place the unmolded pudding on a glass platter drizzled with evaporated milk, then top the pudding with fresh fruits. This refreshing dessert is found in various forms on dim sum dessert carts today.

2 tablespoons unflavored gelatin
½ cup water
1 cup sugar
1 cup boiling water
3 cups mango purée, defrosted if frozen
¾ cup evaporated milk

GARNISHES
Sweetened whipped cream (optional)
Evaporated milk (optional)
Mango slices or green or yellow kiwi slices

Sprinkle gelatin over the water to soften in medium bowl; let stand 5 minutes. Add sugar and boiling water; stir until gelatin and sugar are dissolved. Set aside to cool.

Stir mango purée into cooled gelatin mixture; add milk and stir until ingredients are well-blended. Divide the mixture among 6 to 8 individual dessert dishes (clear or white dishes are preferred so the pretty color of the mango is shown). Refrigerate until set, about 3 to 4 hours.

Garnish with sweetened whipped cream or evaporated milk; top with fresh mango or kiwi slices.

COCONUT BUNS

Yeh Jee Bao

MAKES 12 TO 15 BUNS

A delightful mixture of coconut, candied melon, and peanuts encased in a yeast bun makes a great snack or dessert.

FILLING

1¼ cups shredded coconut
1¼ cups chopped candied winter melon
½ cup chopped peanuts
¼ cup sugar
3 tablespoons toasted sesame seeds

1 recipe Bao (Steamed Bun Dough, page 40)
3 tablespoons vegetable oil

To make filling, combine ingredients in a medium bowl.

Prepare Bao according to directions; divide into 12 to 15 portions. Oil hands and flatten pieces of dough to form 3-inch circles. Put about 1½ tablespoons coconut mixture in center of each piece of dough. Form buns by pulling dough up and around filling; pinch edges together to seal.

Place, seam side down, on squares of parchment paper. Cover and let rise until doubled.

Place on rack and steam over boiling water for 10 to 15 minutes.

CHINESE DOUGHNUTS
Jin Dui

MAKES ABOUT 16

The glutinous rice flour, more commonly called by the Japanese name mochiko in Hawai'i, produces a chewy texture for this fried doughnut. Filled with just a small amount of coconut, peanuts, and sugar, Jin Dui is treasured for its satisfying pull. The savory version is called Ham Sui Gok (page 34) and is just as popular. You can fill these round desserts with sweetened black, red, or yellow bean paste. Some feel that it isn't a dim sum experience without this dessert.

DOUGH

1½ cups Chinese slab sugar, substitute brown sugar
1¼ cups hot water
1 teaspoon Shaoxing wine or dry sherry
16 ounces glutinous rice flour, called mochiko in Japanese

FILLING

½ cup grated coconut
½ cup crushed roasted peanuts
3 tablespoons sugar

¾ cup toasted sesame seeds
1 quart vegetable or canola oil

Dissolve brown sugar in hot water; add wine and set aside to cool. Once sugar mixture is cool, gradually stir liquid into flour to make a stiff dough. Do not knead. Shape dough into a roll, 1½-inches in diameter and cut into ½-inch slices; flatten into circles. Combine filling ingredients in a bowl.

Place one tablespoon of filling mixture in center of dough; pinch edges together to seal; roll into a ball, then roll in sesame seeds.

In batches, deep-fry in oil heated to 365°F until golden brown, about 5 to 7 mintues. Press balls against side of pan while frying so balls will expand. Start with just one or two.

Drain on metal rack or paper towels. Best served hot but may also be served lukewarm.

Variation: Fill with sweetened beans (page 91).

My friend's popo (grandmother) made these doughnuts on special occasions and we were always willing to assist in the making of them as well as serve as " taste testers."

—Muriel

SWEET CHINESE PRETZELS

Tong Wan

MAKES ABOUT 2 DOZEN

Crispy, sweet, and fried. Chinese Pretzels are not to be eaten every day, but are a treat. We are not sure why the same pretzel irons are used in Scandinavia, but both desserts are beautiful. Your friends will appreciate your care in making these fried delights. Take care to have the oil at a high temperature as the pretzels will absorb less oil and taste lighter.

1 cup cornstarch, substitute tapioca starch
3 tablespoons all-purpose flour
¼ cup sugar
Dash of salt
1 large egg, beaten
½ cup whole milk, substitute evaporated milk
1 quart vegetable or canola oil

Combine cornstarch, flour, sugar, and salt in large bowl.

A very popular snack in Hawai'i during the fifties, these pretzels were often made and sold by the girls of our club as a fundraiser.
—Muriel

In a separate bowl, combine egg and milk; whisk to combine. Stir liquid mixture into dry mixture; mix thoroughly.

Heat oil to 365°F; heat pretzel/rosette iron in hot oil for about 10 to 15 seconds. Evenly dip hot iron into batter, being careful not to get any batter over the top of the iron. Dip iron back into the hot oil to fry. As soon as the batter starts to expand from the iron, gradually lift iron up and allow pretzel to drop off. When pretzel is light brown on one side, turn to brown other side.

Drain on a metal rack or paper towels. Cool completely and store in airtight container.

Variation: Savory Pretzels: Add 1 tablespoon minced green onion and ¼ cup minced dried shrimp to batter before frying.

SWEET RICE FLOUR DUMPLINGS

Ip Jai

MAKES 12 DUMPLINGS

These attractive little bundles can be savory or sweet. Wrapped cylinders with oiled ti leaves, the small presents inside are a steamed sticky rice flour outside with sweet coconut, melon, and sesame seeds inside. Also enjoy the savory Ip Jai *(page 80).*

10 ounces glutinous rice flour
1 cup water
¼ cup vegetable oil, divided
⅔ cup chopped candied coconut
⅔ cup chopped candied melon
1½ tablespoons roasted sesame seeds
12 ti leaves*, cut into 7 × 3-inch strips

Mix flour, water, and 2 tablespoons of the oil to make soft dough; divide into 12 portions.

Combine coconut, melon, sesame seeds, and remaining oil; form into 12 balls.

Flatten and mold each portion of dough around a ball of filling. Bring edges together and close top. Oil ti leaf strips; place a ball at one end of strip, fold edge in about 1-inch, and roll up. Place in bowl and steam 40 to 45 minutes.

*May substitute banana or lotus leaves.

CHINESE FLOWER CAKES
Gai Dan Gou

MAKES ABOUT 6 CAKES

These beautifully shaped cakes were sold in Chinatown. The almond flavoring and delicate texture made these a favorite. I remember seeing the baking tins at my grandmother's home. This baked version of a sponge cake is just a perfect way to end a multi-course Chinese meal.

Oil and flour to prepare cake tins
2 cups sifted cake flour
2 teaspoons baking powder
¼ teaspoon salt
1 cup shortening
1½ cups powdered sugar
4 large eggs
2 teaspoons almond extract
½ cup milk

Oil and flour six baking tins (substitute heat-resistant bowls like baking glass bowls about 5 inches in diameter).

Preheat oven to 325°F. Combine cake flour, baking powder, and salt; set aside. In a standing mixer, cream the shortening and sugar for 2 minutes. Add eggs one by one and continue creaming until light in texture, about 5 minutes. Add almond extract and mix 30 seconds. Add flour mixture in three batches to butter mixture, alternating it with milk. Pour mixture into your prepared tins or bowls. Bake until done, about 25 minutes. Test with a bamboo skewer or cake tester. When the skewer comes out clean, cake is done. Cool in the tins for 15 minutes. Use a butter knife to loosen the sides. Flip out using your hands and cool completely on a cooling rack, about 1 hour. Serve simply as is or with ice cream or whipped cream and cut fruit.

STEAMED SPONGE CAKE
Jing Dan Gou

MAKES ABOUT 9 PIECES

A simple but delicious cake which may be served as a dessert as well as a snack—especially good with hot tea. Chinese enjoy their steamed cakes. The tradition of steaming in woks could have started because most homes did not have ovens.

1 cup cake flour
½ teaspoon baking powder
¼ teaspoon salt
5 large eggs, separated
1 cup sugar, divided in half
1 teaspoon lemon extract
3 tablespoons Sweet Bean Filling*

Sift flour, baking powder, and salt together in medium bowl; set aside.

In separate bowl, beat egg whites until foamy. Gradually add ½ cup sugar, continuing to beat until stiff and glossy.

In separate bowl, beat egg yolks until thick and lemon-colored, gradually adding remaining ½ cup sugar and lemon extract.

Fold beaten egg yolks into beaten egg whites. Sprinkle flour mixture over egg mixture in four additions. Fold lightly after each addition. Pour into 8-inch square cake pan and steam 40 minutes.

Cut steamed cake in half, crosswise, to make 2 layers. Spread soybean filling between layers.

Cut into diamond shapes through 2 layers, if desired.

*Sweet Bean Filling is made from soybeans and brown sugar and is sold in Chinese cake shops. You may enjoy black, red beans, or yellow beans sold in Asian markets. Recipe on page 91.

PEANUT-SESAME CANDY

Fa Sung Tong

MAKES ABOUT 2 DOZEN (3-INCH) BARS

Since the 2008 closing of Kwong On in Kaimuki, many miss their Sesame Peanut Candy. Although their recipe is a closely-guarded secret, an old colleague shares her version of this delicious confection.

—Muriel

2 pounds packed brown sugar, dark or light
1/4 cup white vinegar
1/4 cup water
1 3/4 pounds roasted, shelled peanuts
1 cup toasted sesame seeds
Peanut or vegetable oil

In saucepan, mix sugar, vinegar, and water; stir to dissolve. Bring mixture to a boil and cook until thick. Add peanuts and mix well to coat evenly.

Pour mixture into a lightly greased 9 × 13-inch pan sprinkled with one-half of the sesame seeds; flatten mixture by rolling a bottle greased with peanut or vegetable oil to keep the candy from sticking to it. Sprinkle top with remaining sesame seeds. Cool.

Cut into rectangles. Keep in an airtight container.

Variation: Substitute 1 3/4 pounds roasted macadamia nuts, whole or large pieces, for peanuts.

ALMOND COOKIES
Hung Yun Bang

MAKES 24 TO 30

This recipe closely duplicates the authentic Chinese cookies which are often served with Chinese meals. Since the average Chinese home in China did not have an oven, most pastries and cookies were purchased from cake shops. You must use shortening, not butter, to achieve the distinctive texture of these flaky cookies.

- 2¼ cups all-purpose flour
- 1 teaspoon baking soda
- ¼ teaspoon salt
- 1 cup butter-flavored shortening
- ¾ cup sugar
- 1 large egg, at room temperature
- 1 tablespoon almond extract
- Red food coloring or 30 blanched whole almonds

Preheat oven to 325°F. In a large mixing bowl, mix flour, baking soda, and salt. Set aside. In a standing mixer, mix shortening and sugar until well combined. Add in egg and extract and combine. Add flour mixture in three batches. Divide dough into 24 to 30 uniform balls. Roll the dough into balls between your palms and place on an ungreased cookie sheet. Flatten them with your hands or the bottom of a glass to about ⅜-inch in height. Using a round chopstick, dot the center of the cookie or place a whole, blanched almond in the center. Bake for 20 minutes; check at 18 minutes if making smaller cookies. Cool before serving.

SESAME COOKIES
Gee Ma Bang Jai

MAKES ABOUT 5 DOZEN

These cookies offer a nice change in flavor at the end of a hearty meal... they're delicious as a snack any time of day.

1 cup shortening
1 cup sugar
2 large eggs, beaten
1 teaspoon vanilla extract
2 cups all-purpose flour
½ teaspoon baking soda
¼ teaspoon salt
¾ cup toasted sesame seeds

In a standing mixer, cream shortening with sugar until light and fluffy; add eggs and beat well. Stir in vanilla.

In a separate bowl, combine and whisk together flour, baking soda, and salt; add to creamed mixture and blend ingredients together.

Shape dough into roll, about 1½ inches in diameter. Slice into ¼-inch thick disks; press tops of cookies in sesame seeds.

Place 1-inch apart on ungreased cookie sheet. To keep cookies from spreading, put in freezer or refrigerator for 5 minutes before baking. Bake at 400°F for 10 to 12 minutes or until golden brown. Cool thoroughly; store in airtight container.

FORTUNE COOKIES
Hung Won Bang

MAKES ABOUT 3 DOZEN

Fortune cookies were not invented in China, but they are popular in the United States, especially at Chinese restaurants where these cookies are served at the end of a meal. This untraditional dessert is fun to make and you can get creative in making up your own "fortunes."

1 cup all-purpose flour
1/3 cup sugar
1 large egg, slightly beaten
1 teaspoon vanilla extract
1 cup water

Combine all ingredients in a medium bowl. Prepare 1-inch by 3/8-inch strips of paper fortunes to insert in cookies.

Heat griddle or skillet to 350°F. Place 1 tablespoon batter on griddle; spread in a circular motion with the back of a spoon until a thin 3-inch circle is formed. When bubbles appear, turn cookie over and when both sides are browned, remove from griddle and, while still warm, place paper with written fortune in center. Fold cookie in half then bend in half over edge of bowl to form the distinctive crease of a fortune cookie.

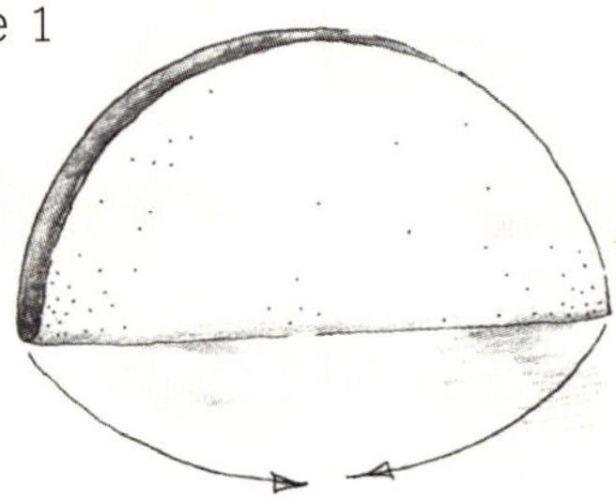

Place in muffin pans to cool. Store in an airtight container.

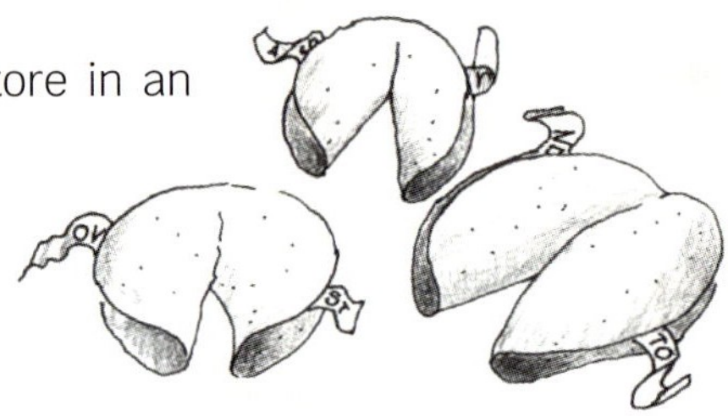

ALMOND FLOAT
Hang Yun Dow Foo

MAKES 4 TO 6 SERVINGS

What could be better than cubes of this light gelatin pudding with sweet canned fruits after a full meal? When younger, we would eat the fruit cocktail in the order of how we preferred the fruit. For me, grapes first and the cherry last!

—Lynette

1 envelope unflavored gelatin
⅓ cup cold water
1 cup hot water
½ cup sugar
½ teaspoon almond extract
½ cup evaporated milk
1 (15-ounce) can fruit cocktail or lychee, optional

In a large mixing bowl, sprinkle gelatin over cold water to soften; let set 5 minutes. Add hot water and sugar; stir to dissolve sugar. Add almond extract and milk. Mix well and pour into a square pan or bowl. Cover with plastic wrap. Refrigerate until set, at least a few hours. Traditionally cut into cubes, but can be scooped in a more informal serving.

Serve with canned fruit cocktail or lychee with syrup.

OTHER DISHES

We expect certain dishes to be served at a restaurant specializing in dim sum. However, each Hawai‘i restaurant may offer other assorted dishes to supplement the smaller dim sum offerings. In these next chapters, we include recipes for some of the popular dishes.

Seafood

Surrounded by the ocean and its bounty, we in Hawai'i savor our seafood. So did southern Chinese living by the rich coastline. So, with strong interest from both Chinese and Hawai'i residents, seafood is one of the most popular items on a menu.

Seafood can be considered dim sum when it is made into a dumpling or other traditional recipes. However, when diners are feeling celebratory, they love to order a seafood dish like Salt and Pepper Shrimp (page 113) to accompany their dim sum. From simple preparations where simple steaming lets the freshness of fish come through (page page 110) to the stronger flavored fermented black bean sauce (page 115), every type of seafood is appreciated.

FISH WITH BLACK BEAN SAUCE

Dow See Jing Yu

MAKES 2 TO 4 SERVINGS

A touch of fermented dow see (fermented black beans) is added to this dish to give it an appealing flavor. Chinese prefer to serve fish whole, showing its head and tail to prove its freshness.

1 whole fresh mullet (about 1 pound), cleaned, substitute 1½ pounds fillet of any white fish

1 tablespoon Hawaiian salt (rock salt)

SEASONINGS

¼ cup dow see (fermented black beans), washed, drained, and crushed

2 tablespoons minced green onion

½ teaspoon minced fresh ginger

½ teaspoon salt

1 tablespoon peanut, vegetable, or canola oil

½ teaspoon sugar

¼ cup water

¼ cup chopped green onion for garnish

Clean, slit sides, and salt fish. Arrange in deep oval or round dish.

Combine seasoning ingredients; mix well and pour over fish.

Steam for 15 minutes or until done. Garnish with green onions to serve.

STEAMED FISH
Jing Yu

MAKES 6 TO 8 SERVINGS

Chinese-style steamed fish is the most popular preparation for fresh fish in Hawaiʻi, bar none. This method of preparation enhances, rather than disguises, the natural flavor of the fish. It is customary to point the head of the fish to the most distinguished guest seated at your table.

1 teaspoon salt
2- to 3-pound whole ʻōpakapaka, ehu, kumu, sea bass, or uhu, scaled and cleaned; substitute any fresh whole fish
2 teaspoons sugar
2 tablespoons soy sauce
3 tablespoons peanut, vegetable, or canola oil, divided
2 tablespoons finely slivered fresh ginger
3 tablespoons chopped green onion
Chinese parsley for garnish

Sprinkle salt inside and over fish; place in shallow heat-resistant dish.

Combine sugar, soy sauce, and 1 tablespoon of the oil; pour over fish. Sprinkle with ginger and green onion. Steam, covered, over boiling water for 15 minutes or until fish is done and begins to flake.

Heat remaining 2 tablespoons oil to almost smoking and pour over fish; garnish with Chinese parsley to serve.

CANTON SHRIMP
Guang Dong Har

MAKES 3 TO 4 SERVINGS

Succulent shrimp served with a flavorful sweet-sour sauce—a popular Chinese dish in Hawai'i.

BATTER
1 cup all-purpose flour
½ teaspoon sugar
1 large egg
½ cup water

½ pound raw shrimp, shelled and deveined
Peanut, vegetable, or canola oil for frying

SWEET SOUR SAUCE
½ cup water
2 tablespoons ketchup
2 tablespoons cider vinegar, substitute white vinegar
2 tablespoons sugar
1 tablespoon toasted sesame seeds, plus additional for garnish
1 tablespoon cornstarch
1 teaspoon Worcestershire sauce
¼ teaspoon salt
Drop of hot sauce

Combine flour and sugar; add egg and water and stir only until flour mixture is moistened.

Dip shrimp into batter and deep-fry in oil heated to 375°F until lightly browned. Drain on paper towels.

Combine Sweet Sour Sauce ingredients in saucepan; simmer over low heat until thickened. Pour over fried shrimp to serve. Garnish with additional sesame seeds, if desired.

SALT AND PEPPER FRIED SHRIMP
Jui Yim Har

MAKES 16 TO 20 PIECES

Piping hot and generously sprinkled with minced garlic and salt and pepper mixture, these shrimp are tasty treats enjoyed by all. Don't forget to provide lots of paper napkins.

1 pound large (16 to 20 count) shrimp, shells on, deveined
3 tablespoons cornstarch
Peanut, vegetable, or canola oil for deep-frying
1 large clove garlic, finely minced
Salt and pepper mixture (page 175), to taste

Rinse and drain shrimp; pat dry with paper towels.

Place cornstarch in zip-top plastic bag; add 8 to 10 shrimp, close top of bag, and shake gently to coat shrimp completely. Repeat to coat all.

In small batches, deep-fry shrimp in oil heated to 350°F for 2 to 3 minutes.

Drain on absorbent paper and toss them with the garlic and generous sprinkling of the salt and pepper mixture. Serve hot.

Variation: Slice 2 jalapeño peppers into rounds, fry them in oil after the shrimp are fried. Sprinkle over shrimp.

BLACK BEAN CLAMS

Dow See Chow Heen

MAKES 4 TO 6 SERVINGS

A quick and easy dish to prepare in less than 20 minutes. Manila clams are the perfect size for this dish, but if you only see the larger, fresh cherrystone clams, try those too.

BLACK BEAN SAUCE

2 teaspoons canola oil
1 clove garlic, minced
1 teaspoon grated fresh ginger
2 teaspoons dow see (fermented black beans), rinsed and smashed
2 tablespoons soy sauce
⅓ cup water
2 tablespoons oyster sauce
¼ cup minced green onion

1 pound fresh clams in shells, cleaned

To make black bean sauce, heat oil in small saucepan over medium heat. Stir-fry garlic and ginger 30 seconds; add remaining ingredients. Bring to a boil. Reduce heat to low.

Add clams and cover. Simmer 2 to 3 minutes or until clam shells open. (Discard any clams that do not open).

Serve hot. The sauce is wonderful over a bowl of hot steaming rice.

Variation: Add ½ pound ground pork with ginger and garlic until browned about 3 to 5 minutes, then add remaining ingredients.

SEAFOOD WITH BLACK BEAN SAUCE

Hoi Seen Dow See

MAKES 4 SERVINGS

Cook a combination of seafood in black bean sauce made from "scratch" for the authentic flavor of Southern China.

- 2 tablespoons dow see (fermented black beans), soaked in water for 5 minutes
- 2 pounds of a combination of shrimp, clams, scallops, or lobster tail
- 1½ tablespoons peanut, vegetable, or canola oil
- 1 clove garlic, minced
- 2 teaspoons minced fresh ginger
- 1 tablespoon soy sauce
- 1 tablespoon Shaoxing wine or dry sherry
- 1½ teaspoons sugar
- ½ teaspoon salt
- Dash of pepper
- ⅓ cup water
- 1 tablespoon cornstarch
- 2 tablespoons water
- ⅓ cup chopped green onions or cut in 1-inch lengths

Drain soaked dow see; mash with spoon and set aside.

Rinse seafood, leaving shells on; drain. If using lobster, cut tail with shell into 2-inch pieces.

Heat oil in wok or skillet; add seafood and sauté for 1 minute.

Combine dow see, garlic, ginger, soy sauce, wine, sugar, salt, pepper, and the ⅓ cup water; stir to mix and add to seafood; cook for 2 minutes, stirring constantly.

Combine cornstarch and 2 tablespoons water to make paste; add to seafood and cook until sauce thickens. Stir in green onions; serve immediately.

Variation: Before adding cornstarch mixture, add 2 large scrambled eggs to mixture, until just cooked, about 2 minutes, then add cornstarch mixture and green onions.

Pork and Beef

Pork is the favorite meat of southern Chinese as pigs could thrive even on hilly terrain and not-ideal lands. When you say meat (yuk), many will think you are speaking about pork. Chinese in Hawai'i appreciate fresh pork belly slabs roasted (Siu Jee Yuk), ground (Jing Jee Yuk), made into sausage (lap cheong), stir-fried with vegetables, or with sweetened (hoisin or sweet and sour) sauces.

In Hawai'i, beef is used sparingly in Chinese dishes: a bit to stir-fry with vegetables. Innards are enjoyed as a staple of dim sum cuisine—leaf and honeycomb tripe and simmered beef tendon.

SWEET SOUR PORK

Tim Tsin Yuk

MAKES 6 TO 8 SERVINGS

This is a Chinese comfort food. Familiar, delicious and full of great tasting sweet and sour gravy. Perfect to feed to a large family. For those of you who prefer your meat boneless. Just make a large pot of rice and enjoy.

1½ pounds pork shoulder or butt, cut into 1-inch cubes
2 teaspoons salt
1 teaspoon Shaoxing wine or dry sherry
2 teaspoons soy sauce
¼ cup cornstarch
3 tablespoons peanut, vegetable, or canola oil

SAUCE
½ cup packed brown sugar
⅔ cup cider vinegar
2 tablespoons ketchup
½ cup pineapple liquid (from canned pineapple)
2 teaspoons soy sauce
1 tablespoon cornstarch dissolved in ¼ cup water

Canned pineapple tidbits or chunks for garnish

Combine pork, salt, wine, soy sauce, and cornstarch; let stand 10 minutes.

In a wok or skillet, heat oil on medium high heat and brown pork in batches until golden brown. Return all browned pork, cover and simmer over moderate heat for 15 minutes. Skim and discard excess fat.

Make the sauce by adding brown sugar, vinegar, ketchup, pineapple liquid and soy sauce to the pork; bring to a boil. Add cornstarch mixture. Heat until cornstarch has thickened, about 3 minutes. Add pineapple chunks if using and cook 2 more minutes. Serve immediately. This dish is easily frozen to enjoy another day.

CRISPY ROAST PORK

Siu Jee Yuk

MAKES 12 TO 18 SERVINGS

Chinese-style belly pork is one of the most decadent, sought-after meats in Hawai'i. Under the intense heat, the skin turns crispy and crunchy. The meat is tender and nicely flavored with salt, sugar, soy sauce, and Chinese Five Spice Powder. In Hong Kong, it is served in delicate cubes. In Hawai'i, we expect it to be a larger piece that can fit nicely in a steamed bao with hoisin or plum sauce. Once you make this simple recipe, you may not stand in line in Chinatown any longer.

3 pounds belly pork with skin*

MARINADE

2 tablespoons Hawaiian salt
1 teaspoon brown sugar
½ teaspoon Chinese Five Spice powder
2 teaspoons Chinese bean sauce (min see)
1 tablespoon soy sauce

SKIN DRY RUB

1 teaspoon baking soda

Clean belly pork and remove any hairs with tweezers. Mix marinade ingredients and rub on the meat-side of the pork. Place on baking tray with sides as there will be excess liquid. Place skin side up and rub baking soda on the skin only. Refrigerate uncovered overnight.

As youngsters, we would get scolded for picking just the crunchy skin from a platter of siu jee yuk.
—Lynette

THE NEXT DAY:

With paper towels and water, remove baking soda from the skin. Wipe three times so all baking soda is removed or meat will be bitter.

Do not remove marinade from the meat-side of pork.

Using a paring knife, stab the skin and make as many punctures as you can. Insert 4 to 5 metal barbecue sticks through the center of the meat to keep it flat.

Place pork on rack in roasting pan filled with ½-inch water. Bake at 425°F for 1 hour 20 minutes or until done and skin is crisp and blistered. Cool at least 45 minutes before cutting into pieces. Hong Kong-style is to serve it in small ½-inch by ½-inch squares. Hawai'i style is the larger the piece the better! Great with steamed Bao buns (page 40), hoisin sauce, and slivered green onions and cucumbers.

*Pork belly, or belly pork as it is also called, will be a delicious preparation if you do not have the skin. However, many people will be disappointed not to have the crispy bits.

STEAMED PORK HASH

Jing Jee Yuk

MAKES ABOUT 4 SERVINGS

This simple homestyle dish is a favorite of my family. The term pork hash can mean two dishes; Siu Mai dumplings or a platter of seasoned ground meat. Both are popular dishes. I remember my paternal grandmother, Louise Ho Lo, selecting the best and fattiest chunks of pork in Chinatown for this dish. At home, she would use two cleavers to make her own ground pork for this savored dish.

—Lynette

1 pound ground pork
½ cup minced water chestnuts
¼ cup minced green onions
2 tablespoons minced dried and salted turnip (chung choy)
1 large egg, slightly beaten
1 tablespoon soy sauce
2 teaspoons cornstarch
2 teaspoons oyster sauce
2 teaspoons Shaoxing wine or dry sherry
1 teaspoon sugar
½ teaspoon salt
Chinese parsley leaves and minced green onion for garnish

Combine all ingredients, except garnishes in medium mixing bowl; mix well. Form mixture into large patty and place on a shallow heat-resistant dish.

Steam for 25 minutes or until done.

Garnish as desired and may be served with soy sauce.

VARIATIONS

- Place 1½-inch piece salted fish (ham yu), soaked in water for 1 hour, on patty before steaming. Or place salted duck yolks (ham dan) on patty before steaming.
- Or rehydrate 2 black mushrooms in hot water, discard stems, and mince caps. Add to mixture before steaming.
- Add ⅛ cup dried shrimp or dried scallops after soaking them in hot water, into the pork mixture.

Steamed pork hash happens to be one of my favorite Chinese comfort foods. It can be ready for steaming within minutes and this mixture can also be used as a filling for a variety of Chinese dishes—stuffed tofu, stuffed eggplant, dumplings, buns, spring rolls, and more!

—Muriel

STIR-FRIED PORK AND VEGETABLES
Mu Shu Yuk

MAKES 4 SERVINGS

Mu Shu is a Northern Chinese dish, not Southern, but has proved popular and now is served in many restaurants. Mu Shu with pork is traditional, but you can use chicken, lamb, or beef strips. Some restaurants mix in scrambled eggs. To keep this dish vegan, use very firm tofu and substitute vegetable broth instead of chicken broth.

Using Asian vegetables of bamboo shoots, black mushrooms, tree fungus, and carrots keep the mu shu light and flavorful. As is the Chinese way, a minimal amount of meat is added for flavor.

- ½ pound lean pork
- 1 cup slivered bamboo shoots
- 4 dried black mushrooms, soaked in hot water until tender; parboiled
- 4 large tree fungus (elephant ears, pepeiao), soaked and cleaned
- 1 small carrot, pared
- ½ cup cornstarch, divided use
- ½ cup soy sauce
- ½ cup vegetable oil
- 2 teaspoons minced garlic
- 2 teaspoons brown sugar
- 2 teaspoons sesame oil
- 2 teaspoons white pepper
- 2 tablespoons Shaoxing wine or dry sherry
- 1 tablespoon dow jien (Sichuan hot bean paste)
- ½ cup chicken broth
- Salt to taste

Julienne cut pork, bamboo shoots, mushrooms, tree fungus, and carrot into the size of matchsticks. Set aside on a plate, but keep separated.

Sprinkle 1 tablespoon cornstarch and soy sauce over pork; mix and let stand 1 to 2 minutes.

Heat vegetable oil over medium flame in wok; stir-fry pork 1 to 2 minutes; add garlic and stir-fry additional minute. Add brown sugar, sesame oil, white pepper, wine, and hot bean paste. Add chicken broth gradually as needed. Add enough chicken broth to remaining cornstarch to make thin paste; add just enough to vegetable mixture to thicken; cook until starch is cooked and gravy is translucent, 1 to 2 minutes. Add salt to taste.

Wrap Mu Shu Pork in Mandarin Pancakes (page 54).

Variation: Substitute slivered chicken thighs or extra firm tofu for pork.

BARBECUED PORK

Char Siu

MAKES ABOUT 1 POUND

One could argue that this is the favorite way for Chinese to prepare meat. Southern Chinese prefer pork over beef. The meat is marinated and then roasted for a sweet flavor throughout the pork. Start with a piece that has some fat such as shoulder or butt and even belly pork. If you use a leaner cut, the finished product will be too dry. Char Siu has become part of what Hawai'i people consider "favorite local foods". Versions of it appear on the menus of many restaurants. It is a favorite ingredient in dim sum, in fried noodles and just eaten as a snack.

MARINADE

1/4 cup soy sauce
1/4 cup honey
1/4 cup hoisin sauce
1 tablespoon Shaoxing wine or dry sherry
1/4 teaspoon salt
1/2 teaspoon Chinese Five Spice powder
1/4 teaspoon red food coloring, optional
Optional: additional honey as glaze

1 1/2 pounds pork shoulder or butt, not lean such as tenderloin, cut into thick strips (approximately 1 1/2 × 1 1/2 × 5 inches)

Combine marinade ingredients; mix well and rub on pork to coat evenly. Cover with plastic wrap and marinate in refrigerator 1 to 2 nights, turning occasionally.

Place on rack in shallow roasting pan lined with foil and roast at 350°F for 45 minutes to 1 hour or until done. Brush additional honey on meat before serving, if desired.

Slice thinly and serve hot or at room temperature. This recipe is easily doubled. Keep frozen after roasting and use for noodles, bao or to enjoy by itself.

SWEET SOUR SPARERIBS

Tim Tsin Pai Gwat

MAKES 6 SERVINGS

Always one of the favorite dishes at a Chinese dinner, following is a simple recipe that makes it easy to prepare this dish at home. It is even better made the day before serving.

1 tablespoon soy sauce
2 tablespoons flour
2 pounds pork spareribs, cut in 1½-inch pieces
3 tablespoons vegetable oil
1 clove garlic, crushed
1-inch piece fresh ginger, crushed
1½ cups water
⅔ cup cider vinegar
1 cup packed light brown sugar
2 teaspoons salt

Sprinkle soy sauce and flour over spareribs; mix well.

In a large wok or sauce pan, add oil and brown spareribs in batches with garlic and ginger, about 5 minutes; drain and discard fat. Repeat until done.

Add remaining ingredients; simmer on low heat until tender, about 45 minutes. Serve with steamed rice.

CANTONESE RIBS
Pai Gwat

MAKES 10 TO 12 SERVINGS

When a meat dish is called Cantonese-style, this brings to mind a sweet marinade with soy sauce, ketchup, liquor, and sugar. Roasted on a low heat until tender and shiny, these can be enjoyed any season of the year.

MARINADE

1/2 cup soy sauce
1/2 cup packed light brown sugar
1/2 cup ketchup
1/2-inch piece fresh ginger, peeled and crushed
2 tablespoons Shaoxing wine or dry sherry
1/2 teaspoon salt
1 large clove garlic, crushed

3 pounds pork loin back ribs

Combine marinade ingredients; mix thoroughly. Retain 1/4 cup marinade for basting. Rub the remaining marinade onto ribs and refrigerate overnight.

Place ribs on a rack placed on a roasting pan filled with 1/2-inch of water to catch the dripping fat. Baste occasionally while roasting at 325°F for 1 hour or until done. Roast longer if you like the meat "falling off the bone." Cut between ribs to serve.

BAKED HOISIN RIBS
Hoy Tsin Pai Gwat

MAKES 6 TO 8 SERVINGS

This easy recipe just takes three ingredients to make Chinese-style sweet pork spareribs.

2 racks pork spareribs
15 ounces hoisin sauce
15 ounces honey

Remove excess fat and tissues from ribs; brush hoisin sauce on both sides and let stand in refrigerator uncovered overnight.

Place pork ribs on baking sheets lined with foil; brush with honey on one side. Bake at 350°F for 30 minutes; turn, brush with honey on other side and bake additional 30 minutes or until done. Cook longer if you like your meat more tender.

Brush honey on both sides and leave in oven additional 5 minutes to glaze. Remove from oven; let stand 5 minutes; cut into desired sizes to serve.

CURRIED BEEF
Ga Lei Ngau Yuk

MAKES 4 TO 6 SERVINGS

Curry made its way into Chinese cuisine from trading with India. These spices go well with the richness of beef.

MARINADE

3 tablespoons soy sauce
2 tablespoons peanut, vegetable, or canola oil
1 tablespoon sugar
1½ teaspoons cornstarch

---

2 pounds sirloin or tri-tip steak, sliced into thin strips
3 tablespoons peanut, vegetable, or canola oil
1 onion, sliced
1 clove garlic, minced
1½ teaspoons minced fresh ginger
½ cup water
2 tablespoons yellow curry powder
1 tablespoon cornstarch
¼ teaspoon salt

Combine marinade ingredients. Add beef; mix well and marinate 30 minutes.

Heat 3 tablespoons oil in wok or large skillet; stir-fry onion, garlic, and ginger for 1 minute.

Add beef with marinade and stir-fry additional 2 minutes.

Mix water, curry powder, cornstarch, and salt into beef mixture. Cook over medium heat, stirring constantly, until mixture thickens. Serve with steamed rice or with fried noodles.

Variation: Add one large tomato, cut into sections when you stir-fry the onion, garlic, and ginger.

BEEF TENDON BEEF STEW WITH TURNIP

Ngau Nam Ngau Yuk

MAKES 10 TO 12 SERVINGS AS A MAIN DISH

This is an old-fashioned stew that highlights the love for the unique texture of beef tendons and shank meat. At many dim sum houses, it is offered as a popular hot pot dish. Turnip chunks absorb the earthy flavors from nam yue (red fermented tofu sauce). This is a strong flavored dish that can feed many; just make a huge pot of rice.

2½ pounds beef tendon
1½ pounds beef shank, beef flank or boneless short ribs
3 tablespoons oil
2 inches ginger, peeled and sliced
1 tablespoon minced garlic
2 tablespoon white stem of green onion, chopped
½ cup soy sauce
3 tablespoons Chinese bean sauce
3 tablespoons fermented red bean curd (nam yue)
2 tablespoons chopped green onion, plus more for garnish
1½ tablespoons hoisin sauce
1½ tablespoons oyster sauce
2 tablespoons broken Chinese slab sugar, substitute brown sugar
2½ pounds Chinese turnip, peeled and cut into 1½-inch chunks, substitute daikon or Korean turnip
3 tablespoons cornstarch mixed with ¼ cup water (optional)
Chopped green onions for garnish

Bring 10 cups water to boil in a large stock pot. Add tendon and boil for 10 minutes, remove and cool. In same water, boil meat for 10 minutes, remove and cool. Drain water and add oil. On high heat, add ginger, garlic, and green onions. Then add soy sauce, bean sauce, red bean curd, green onion, hoisin, oyster sauce, and sugar. Add 8 cups water. Cut tendon in 2-inch chunks and add to pot. Bring to a boil, then reduce heat to low and cover for 1 hour. Cut meat into 1½-inch chunks and add to pot. Bring to a boil, then reduce to low, cover and cook for 1 hour. Add turnip chunks and cook 1 hour longer. Check for tenderness of all three ingredients. If necessary, remove meat and turnip if tendon needs additional time and continue to cook until tender. Skim and discard oil. Remove ginger slices. If you want a thicker gravy, add constarch and water mixture. Continue to stir over medium-low heat until liquid thickens. Garnish with green onions. Best served hot. Great if cooked the day before, cooled and refrigerated.

OYSTER SAUCE BEEF WITH SNOW PEAS

Lan Dow Ngau Yuk

MAKES ABOUT 6 SERVINGS

Traditionally, vegetables comprised most of this dish and just a small amount of meat was used for flavor. This recipe reflects our American love of meat. Oyster sauce flavors the beef and the snow peas are added just at the last moment, so they retain their crunch. Serve over steamed rice or noodles for an easy meal.

1½ pounds beef, such as flank steak, thinly sliced against the grain

MARINADE

1 tablespoon cornstarch
1 tablespoon sugar
1¼ teaspoons soy sauce
2 teaspoons Shaoxing wine or dry sherry
¼ cup oyster sauce
2 tablespoons peanut, vegetable, or canola oil, divided

¼ cup thinly sliced onion
1 clove garlic, minced
2 cups snow peas, strings removed

Combine sliced beef, cornstarch, sugar, soy sauce, wine, oyster sauce, and 1 tablespoon of the oil; marinate for 20 minutes.

Brown onion in hot remaining oil; add beef and garlic; stir-fry for 1 minute. Add peas and cook an additional minute. Serve hot.

Chicken and Duck

Chinese enjoy poultry. Chicken and duck are especially appreciated in Hawaiʻi. Growing up, we would fight over the innards—heart, gizzard, and liver. The entire bird and especially wings are more popular with the mainstream audiences. Fried pieces are devoured at family parties. Duck doesn't have to be a special occasion food. You can prepare it at home easily and serve the delicacies with Mandarin Pancakes or Steamed Bao.

CRISPY CHICKEN WINGS
Chui Pei Gai Yick

MAKES 10 TO 12 SERVINGS AS AN APPETIZER

Chicken wings seem to be popular in any preparation. Quickly marinated, then battered and fried, these will be eaten quickly at your parties.

2 pounds chicken wings

MARINADE

- 2 tablespoons soy sauce
- 2 tablespoons Shaoxing wine or dry sherry
- 2 teaspoons salt
- 2 teaspoons sugar
- 1 teaspoon fresh ginger juice (grate fresh ginger, then squeeze for juice)
- 1 large clove garlic, crushed

BATTER

- ½ cup flour
- ½ cup cornstarch
- 2 large eggs, beaten
- ¾ cup water

1 quart vegetable or canola oil for frying

Cut off wing tips (use them later to make chicken broth). Cut into remaining two parts at joint.

Combine marinade ingredients in resealable plastic bag; add chicken and marinate at least 1 hour or overnight.

Combine flour and cornstarch in mixing bowl. Combine beaten eggs with water and add to flour mixture. Stir just until mixed; batter will be lumpy.

Dip chicken wings in batter. Deep fry in oil heated to 365°F until golden brown, about 4 to 5 minutes. Drain on paper towels. Serve hot with a spiced dip of your choice (page 170).

SPICY FRIED CHICKEN
Heung Lat Ja Ji Gai

MAKES 12 TO 16 SERVINGS

Fried chicken with a spicy sauce. What could be better for an appetizer or snack? The unusual technique in this recipe is flavoring the chicken right after it is fried, by dipping it in the hot sauce. Yes. You will want to lick your fingers.

4 pounds chicken wings
3 cups all-purpose flour
1 quart vegetable or canola oil for deep-frying

SAUCE
½ cup soy sauce
½ cup sugar
¼ cup water
2 tablespoons minced green onion
½ teaspoon minced garlic
1 small Hawaiian chili pepper, seeded and minced
¼ teaspoon grated fresh ginger

Chopped green onions for garnish

Pat-dry chicken with paper towel; cut off wing tips (save for making chicken stock) and cut to separate middle section from drumette. Dredge in flour and deep fry in oil heated to 365°F until golden brown and cooked through, about 8 to 10 minutes. Drain on paper towels.

Combine ingredients for sauce; mix well and dip chicken into sauce while hot. Arrange on serving platter. Garnish with green onions. Serve any additional sauce on side. May be served hot or cold.

SOY SAUCE CHICKEN
See Yau Gai

MAKES 6 SERVINGS

Star Anise, liquor, ginger, and garlic make this Chinese preparation different from the Japanese version. This is a simple preparation that is a classic offering. Like with most recipes, the fresher the chicken, the better the dish.

¼ cup peanut, vegetable, or canola oil
2-inch piece fresh ginger, peeled and crushed
2 large cloves garlic, crushed
8 star anise
1 (3- to 4-pound) fresh whole chicken, dressed and cut into pieces
½ cup soy sauce
½ cup water
3 tablespoons brown sugar
1 tablespoon Shaoxing wine or dry sherry
Chinese parsley for garnish

Heat oil, ginger, garlic, and star anise in a wok or skillet on medium-high heat. Add chicken pieces and fry until slightly brown.

Add mixture of soy sauce, water, sugar, and wine. Cover and cook on medium low heat until tender. Turn chicken from time to time to get an even brown. Check for doneness after 40 minutes. Serve hot with juices. Garnish with Chinese parsley.

Use dry sherry as a substitution for Chinese Shaoxing wine. A sweet sherry is not a good substitute.

POT ROAST CHICKEN
Mun Gai

MAKES 4 TO 6 SERVINGS

This dish will soon become one of your favorites as it is easy to prepare and is ready to serve in less than an hour. Delicious with hot steamed rice!

- 3 pounds chicken thighs, boneless, skin-on or skinless
- ½ teaspoon salt
- ⅓ cup soy sauce
- 1½ tablespoons peanut, vegetable, or canola oil
- 4 dried black mushrooms, soaked in hot water and drained
- ½-inch piece fresh ginger, crushed
- 2 tablespoons Shaoxing wine or dry sherry
- ½ cup snow peas, strings removed
- 2 green onions, cut into 1-inch lengths
- 1 tablespoon cornstarch dissolved in ¾ cup water
- 1 tablespoon soy sauce
- 1 teaspoon sugar
- Chinese parsley leaves or chopped green onions for garnish

Rub chicken with salt and soy sauce; let stand 10 to 15 minutes.

Brown chicken in hot oil in a wok or skillet on all sides over high heat; discard mushroom stems and cut each cap into four wedges and add to wok.

Combine ginger and wine; pour over chicken and mushrooms. Cover and simmer over low heat for 30 minutes or until chicken is tender.

Transfer chicken to serving dish, leaving mushrooms in skillet. Add remaining ingredients to mushrooms except parsley; cook until sauce thickens. Pour sauce over chicken; garnish and serve immediately.

GINGER CHICKEN
Bak Chit Gai

MAKES 10 TO 12 SERVINGS

This dish is enjoyed cold or hot. It is fresh chicken simply cooked with a ginger-garlic-green onion sauce.

5 cups water
1½ teaspoons salt
3½ pounds fresh whole fryer chicken
Vegetable oil to coat chicken
Won bok cabbage for plating

GINGER SAUCE
2 tablespoons minced Chinese parsley
2 tablespoons minced green onion
2 tablespoons minced fresh ginger
1 clove garlic, finely minced
3 tablespoons peanut, vegetable, or canola oil
Salt to taste

In a large pot, combine water and salt; bring to a boil. Add whole chicken and simmer 20 to 25 minutes. Remove chicken and cool. Rub entire chicken skin with oil so it is not dry.

Cut chicken into serving pieces and arrange attractively on platter lined with cooked won bok cabbage, if desired. Serve immediately or refrigerate.

Combine Ginger Sauce ingredients except oil; mix well. Heat oil until smoking and pour over the rest of the sauce ingredients. Add salt to taste. Serve alongside chilled or room-temperature chicken or pour sauce on cut chicken.

Variation: Hot Chicken: Gently heat chicken in a steamer. Be careful not to overcook chicken. Heat sauce in a sauce pan. Pour sauce over chicken.

PEKING DUCK (WESTERN-STYLE)

Bak Ging Aap

MAKES 4 TO 6 SERVINGS

Peking Duck is named for the Chinese city and the true method of preparation requires a day or more and some unique techniques. Only the skin of the duck was originally intended for consumption but today, everyone eats the meat too—either as is or stir-fried with vegetables and served as an additional dish. Later, the bones can be simmered into a delicious soup with vegetables. This version requires only a few hours of preparation and it is seasoned and roasted in a simple manner which yields moist, succulent meat and tasty, crispy skin.

1 (4½ to 5 pound) duck, defrosted, if frozen
½ teaspoon ground ginger
½ teaspoon ground cinnamon
¼ teaspoon ground white pepper
Dash ground cloves
1 tablespoon soy sauce
2 teaspoons honey
Chinese parsley, for garnish
Steamed buns (page 40)
4 green onions, cut into thin diagonal slices
½ cup Chinese plum or hoisin sauce

Rinse inside and outside of duck; pat dry with paper towel and reserve giblets for other uses.

Mix ginger, cinnamon, pepper, and cloves; dust ½ teaspoon of this mixture inside duck. Rub remaining spice mixture evenly over duck exterior. Close abdominal cavity with skewers. Wrap with foil, folding edges to seal securely.

Place duck in large baking pan. Bake at 425°F for 1 hour.

Remove from oven and let stand 20 minutes or until slightly cooled. Carefully open foil at one end and drain out the accumulated juices and fat; discard foil.

Set duck on rack in baking pan and prick skin lightly with a knife or fork. Return to oven. Bake at 375°F for 30 minutes.

Combine soy sauce with honey; brush onto duck. Return to oven. Bake at 500°F for 5 minutes or until nicely browned; do not burn.

Separate skin from meat and place on serving platter; garnish with Chinese parsley.

To eat, serve small sliced pieces of crisp skin and meat on steamed bun (page 40). Top with green onion slices, Chinese parsley, and a dab of plum or hoisin sauce.

ROAST DUCK
Siu Aap

MAKES 6 TO 8 SERVINGS

The rich taste of seasoned duck is popular in Hawai'i. Chinese flavors of five spice powder, ginger, and honey combine to make a winning dish that is easy to prepare at home.

4- to 5-pound duck, defrosted if frozen

SEASONING

1 tablespoon Shaoxing wine or dry sherry
2 teaspoons Chinese Five Spice powder
2 teaspoons kosher salt
½ teaspoon white pepper
1 teaspoon sugar
1-inch piece ginger, peeled and crushed
2 stalks green onions, tied in a knot

GLAZE

½ cup boiling water
2 tablespoons honey

Clean duck and wipe dry. In a bowl, combine seasoning ingredients. Use a brush to coat cavity of duck with the seasoning mixture (not the skin). Insert ginger and green onions in cavity of duck. Refrigerate overnight in an uncovered baking pan.

Combine glaze ingredients and pour over duck, rubbing to spread evenly.

Place duck on wire rack and roast at 325°F for 1 hour and 20 minutes or until done. Cut into pieces and serve on platter over a bed of blanched vegetables such as baby bok choy, won bok cabbage, or mustard cabbage. Serve with plum or hoisin sauce.

Alternatively, cut the skin and meat into slices and serve with steamed Bao (page 40), slivered green onions, and slices of cucumber. Or serve on a bed of Seasoned Peanuts (page 84)

LEMON CHICKEN

Ning Mung Gai

MAKES 4 TO 6 SERVINGS

Fried chicken bites with a contrasting citrus sauce proves to be a popular combination. Change it from the usual by using fresh oranges instead of lemons.

MARINADE

½ teaspoon salt
1 tablespoon Shaoxing wine or dry sherry
1 tablespoon soy sauce

1 pound boneless chicken breasts, cut in bite-sized pieces

BATTER

2 large eggs, slightly beaten
¼ cup cornstarch
½ teaspoon baking powder

2 cups peanut, vegetable, or canola oil for frying

LEMON SAUCE

1 tablespoon vegetable oil
1 teaspoon salt
3 tablespoons sugar
1 tablespoon cornstarch
2 tablespoons fresh lemon juice
1 cup chicken broth

1 to 2 lemons, sliced thinly in rounds for garnish

Combine marinade ingredients in resealable bag. Add chicken and marinate for 15 minutes.

Combine batter ingredients; beat to form a smooth mixture. Coat chicken pieces with batter and deep-fry in oil heated to 365°F for 4 to 5 minutes or until brown. Drain on absorbent paper.

To prepare Lemon Sauce, heat oil and slowly add remaining ingredients. Stir constantly, cooking over low heat until sauce is thickened and clear. Pour over chicken to serve. Garnish with lemon slices.

Variation: Orange Chicken: Substitute freshly squeezed orange juice and oranges for lemon juice and lemon slices.

Vegetables

When going to yum cha, usually one or two vegetable dishes are ordered, along with dumplings. Greens are especially treasured and are usually stir-fried to keep the vegetables crisp.

Immigrants to Hawai'i from China brought over their favorite vegetables to plant in their gardens. Greens like Chinese broccoli (gai lan), choy sum, mustard cabbage (gai choy), young sprouts from the pea vines (dau miu), bitter melon, snow peas, and squash are savored with a variety of flavorings. Even the humble celery is enjoyed in a stir-fry. Ask for shrimp, dried and fresh scallops, dried and fresh fish, strips of beef, pork, or chicken to add to the freshest vegetable of the day.

Standard stir-fries use sauces with spicy soy sauce or simply oil and garlic. Whatever your craving, there is a vegetable for you to enjoy.

CHINESE CHICKEN SALAD
Gai Sa Luk

MAKES 10 TO 12 SERVINGS

This popular salad is refreshing and full of crunch. For the customary mouthfeel, use out-of-favor now, old-fashioned iceberg lettuce. Finely sliced celery adds more texture as does the garnish of wonton strips and roasted peanuts.

SALAD

- 1 pound cooked boneless chicken breast, shredded
- 1 medium head iceberg lettuce, shredded
- ½ cup chopped Chinese parsley
- ¼ cup minced green onion
- ¼ cup thinly sliced celery

SESAME VINEGAR DRESSING

- ⅓ cup rice vinegar
- ¼ cup sugar
- ¼ cup canola oil
- 2 tablespoons toasted sesame seeds
- 1 teaspoon salt
- ½ teaspoon freshly ground pepper

GARNISH

- 3 ounces fried wonton strips
- ¼ cup chopped roasted peanuts
- Chinese parsley leaves (optional)

Combine all salad ingredients in large bowl.

Mix ingredients for sesame vinegar dressing in a jar; cover and shake vigorously. Just before serving, pour dressing over salad; toss gently and garnish with wonton strips and peanuts. Top with Chinese parsley leaves as additional garnish. Serve immediately.

Variation: Reduce chicken to ½ pound and add ½ pound of char siu strips (page 124).

You wouldn't find Chinese Chicken Salad in China years ago. Its invention is credited to Sylvia Wu of Madame Wu's restaurant in Los Angeles, where Hollywood stars like Mae West and Cary Grant would order this salad.

BASIC STIR-FRY FORMULA

MAKES ABOUT 4 TO 6 SERVINGS

What is great about Stir-Fries is there is no wrong combination. Use whatever vegetables you enjoy and combine them with a basic sauce and you have a winning dish. Just make sure you stop cooking before the texture is right as the vegetables will continue to cook.

2 tablespoons peanut, vegetable, or canola oil
1 pound meat, chicken, or seafood
1 to 2 pounds vegetables of choice
1 recipe aromatic base (2 tablespoons minced green onion, 2 teaspoons each of minced garlic and fresh ginger)
1 recipe Stir-Fry Sauce (page 148) of choice

VARIATIONS

- Beef, red bell peppers, onions, and black mushrooms with Spicy Sichuan Sauce (recipe follows).
- Pork, black mushrooms, asparagus, red onions, carrots, and bok choy with Black Bean Sauce (page 114).
- Chicken chunks with white mushrooms, red bell peppers with Cantonese Lemon Sauce (recipe follows).
- Shrimp with green bell peppers, asparagus, sugar snap peas, carrots, and bok choy with purchased oyster sauce.
- Chicken with black mushrooms, broccoli, carrots, and sugar snap peas with Sesame Soy Sauce (recipe follows).

(continued on the next page)

STIR-FRY SAUCES

To prepare the following sauces, whisk together cornstarch with the other ingredients until well-blended; pour into the stir-fry, stirring well to coat evenly and cook until gravy thickens, about 15 seconds. Transfer the stir-fry vegetables to a bowl and serve immediately with hot steamed rice.

SPICY SICHUAN SAUCE

MAKES ABOUT 2/3 CUP

- 1½ teaspoons cornstarch
- 1½ teaspoons soy sauce
- ¼ cup chicken broth
- 2 tablespoons Shaoxing wine or dry sherry
- 1 tablespoon Asian chili paste
- 1 tablespoon minced green onion
- 1 tablespoon hoisin sauce

SESAME-SOY SAUCE

MAKES ABOUT ½ CUP

- 1½ teaspoons cornstarch
- 2 teaspoons rice vinegar
- ⅓ cup chicken broth
- 2 tablespoons soy sauce
- 1 tablespoon sugar
- 1 tablespoon minced green onion
- 2 teaspoons toasted sesame seeds
- 2 teaspoons toasted sesame oil
- ½ teaspoon minced garlic

CANTONESE ORANGE OR LEMON SAUCE

MAKES ABOUT ½ CUP

- 1½ teaspoons cornstarch
- ⅓ cup chicken broth
- 2 tablespoons freshly squeezed lemon or orange juice
- 2 tablespoons Shaoxing wine or dry sherry
- 2 teaspoons soy sauce
- 1½ teaspoons oyster sauce
- 1 teaspoon sugar
- ½ teaspoon minced fresh ginger

CHICKEN BROCCOLI
Gai Sai Laan Faa

MAKES 4 TO 6 SERVINGS

A healthy combination of chicken and broccoli as a side dish, simply seasoned with salt and pepper. This is a nice variation from the usual beef combination.

4 large dried black mushrooms, soaked in hot water 30 minutes
1 tablespoon peanut, vegetable, or canola oil
1 clove garlic, minced
2 cups sliced skinless, boneless chicken breasts or thighs, cut into bite-sized pieces
1 pound broccoli crowns, washed and cleaned
1 teaspoon sesame oil
1 teaspoon salt
Dash of pepper

Drain mushrooms, but retain liquid. Discard stems and cut caps into slices. Heat oil in wok or skillet. Add garlic and stir-fry for 30 seconds. Add chicken and stir-fry 2 to 3 minutes; add remaining ingredients and simmer 3 to 5 minutes or until broccoli is of desired doneness. Add mushroom liquid, if needed. Serve immediately with fried noodles or hot rice.

STIR-FRIED ASPARAGUS WITH BEEF

Ngau Yuk Lou San

MAKES 4 TO 6 SERVINGS

Generations ago, meat was used very sparingly as it was expensive. Vegetables from a home garden were much more plentiful, so the ratio of vegetables to meat was high. Asparagus has such a strong flavor; you can easily substitute extra firm tofu for the beef and still have a tasty dish.

MARINADE

1 tablespoon soy sauce
1 teaspoon sugar
1 teaspoon minced fresh ginger

1 pound flank steak, flatiron, or tri-tip, sliced thinly against the grain
2 tablespoons peanut, vegetable, or canola oil
1½ pounds asparagus, tough stems discarded, cut into 1½-inch lengths at a diagonal
1 tablespoon cornstarch mixed with ¼ cup water
Chinese parsley for garnish

Combine marinade ingredients in a small bowl. Add beef and marinate for 30 minutes. Heat oil in a wok or skillet on high heat. Stir-fry beef 1 minute; add asparagus; continue cooking for 2 minutes.

Make a well in the center of vegetables, then add the cornstarch and water mixture. Cook until gravy comes to a boil, stirring constantly. Serve hot. Garnish with Chinese parsley leaves.

Variation: Instead of beef, substitute 8 ounces cubed, drained extra firm tofu or fried tofu.

GINGER-GARLIC BABY BOK CHOY

Siu Bak Choy

MAKES 4 SERVINGS

This simple stir-fried dish is packed with flavor and makes an excellent side dish. Ginger and dried chilies give it kick.

1¼ teaspoons salt, divided
1 pound baby bok choy
2 tablespoons Shaoxing wine or dry sherry
2 teaspoons oyster sauce
1 teaspoon soy sauce
1 tablespoon vegetable oil
1 tablespoon minced garlic
1 tablespoon minced ginger
3 small dried red chilies

Fill medium saucepan with water; add 1 teaspoon of salt and bring to a boil.

Fill large bowl with cold water. Set aside.

Trim ends off from bok choy, separating and rinsing the leaves as they tend to capture dirt; add to boiling water in saucepan. Blanch bok choy for 1 minute or until color turns bright green. Using slotted spoon, transfer bok choy to cold water to cool. Drain and set aside.

In small bowl, whisk together the wine, oyster sauce, soy sauce, and remaining salt. Set aside.

In large skillet, heat the oil over high heat, swirling the pan to coat all sides. Add garlic, ginger, and chilies; sauté about 10 seconds. Add bok choy and sauce; sauté until the liquid has reduced by half, about 1 to 2 minutes. Serve immediately.

STUFFED BITTER MELON
Yeung Foo Qwa

MAKES 6 TO 8 SERVINGS

If you would like to serve something with a unique flavor, try this vegetable dish stuffed with pork. Chinese will tell you it is good for reducing high-blood pressure and diabetes.

4 large bitter melons
1 pound ground pork
1/4 teaspoon soy sauce
1/2 teaspoon salt
1/4 cup minced green onion
1/2 teaspoon oyster sauce

SAUCE
1 cup water
1 tablespoon peanut, vegetable, or canola oil
1/2 teaspoon shrimp sauce (harm ha)
1/2 teaspoon cornstarch

Cut each melon crosswise into 2-inch lengths and remove all seeds. If you want to mellow the bitter taste, blanch in boiling water for 2 minutes; drain. If you like the flavor stronger, do not blanch.

Combine pork with soy sauce, salt, green onion, and oyster sauce; mix well. Stuff melon with pork mixture.

Combine sauce ingredients in skillet; bring to a boil.

Arrange stuffed melons in skillet in one layer, if possible. Cover and cook over medium heat 20 to 25 minutes or until done. Enjoy hot or at room temperature.

Rice & Noodles

RICE

Rice is the staple of the traditional Chinese diet. Though the basic starch of northern Chinese is noodles and bread, they still eat rice...many love both. I've loved fried rice ever since I was a child when my mother would stir-fry leftover cooked meats with surplus rice from last evening's dinner and on occasion, an egg and diced vegetables would be tossed in to make it a "meal in a bowl." Though the recipes that follow call for some ingredients commonly found in Asian kitchens, the possibilities for improvisation are endless. You can stick with classic Asian ingredients or improvise with some of your own seasonings and ingredients. Fried rice is a delicious, economical, and very satisfying one-dish meal.

NOODLES

In China, noodles are considered a "fabulous food" where you can have both wheat-based egg noodles in the north and rice noodles in the south. Noodles are served hot, cold, stir-fried, deep-fried, just boiled, and even pan-fried.

In Hawai'i, Chinese noodles are considered comfort food by all ethnic groups.

FRIED RICE
Chow Fan

MAKES 6 TO 8 SERVINGS

There are many, many variations of fried rice. Because it is usually made with leftovers, it is a very versatile dish. Following is a basic recipe for this comfort food. Create your own combination of ingredients such as zucchini, fresh herbs, corn, and season it with whatever suits you—dow see (fermented black beans), or even a little fish sauce instead of salt, soy sauce, or oyster sauce.

3 tablespoons vegetable oil
¼ pound raw shrimp, cleaned and minced
½ pound char siu, slivered
2 teaspoons shrimp sauce (harm ha), optional
1 cup bean sprouts, washed and drained, optional
½ cup chopped green onions
¼ cup chopped Chinese parsley
¼ cup frozen peas, defrosted
6 cups cold, cooked rice, long grain rice preferred

SEASONINGS
1 tablespoon soy sauce
1 tablespoon oyster sauce
½ teaspoon salt

2 large eggs, beaten, pan-fried and cut into strips
¼ cup minced green onion
Chopped Chinese parsley, for garnish (optional)

Heat oil in wok. Stir-fry shrimp in wok over high heat, 1 minute. Add char siu, shrimp sauce (if using), bean sprouts, green onions, and Chinese parsley; stir-fry 1 minute; remove to serving dish. Stir in rice to hot wok and add seasoning ingredients; stir-fry an additional minute or until heated through. Add back shrimp mixture, fried egg pieces, and green onion; mix and toss gently to mix thoroughly. Serve sprinkled with additional Chinese parsley, if desired.

Fried Rice Basics:

- Begin with day-old or cold cooked rice. Long grain rice stays separated more than others.
- To dry cooked rice, freeze it for a day.
- Add vegetables and meat or seafood that contrast in flavor, texture, and color. Cut into uniform pieces for even cooking.
- Ginger and curry powder can enhance the flavor of the dish, but use them sparingly so as not to overpower the other flavors.
- Use a non-stick skillet or cast-iron skillet if a well-seasoned wok is not available.
- If a wok is used, make certain that the wok is very hot before adding oil and proceeding with the recipe.

BEEF LONG RICE
Ngau Yuk Fun See

MAKES 8 TO 10 SERVINGS

Long rice is also known as mung bean threads, sai fun, glass noodles, Chinese vermicelli, or cellophane noodles. These thin, dry noodles turn translucent and "glassy" once soaked and softened and they are a delicious addition to soups and some "soupy" casseroles.

1 pound beef such as flank steak, flat iron, tri-tip, sliced
1 tablespoon Shaoxing wine, substitute dry sherry
½ teaspoon salt
3 tablespoons peanut or vegetable oil, divided use
2 stalks celery, sliced thinly, diagonally
1 medium bell pepper, sliced crosswise
1 medium onion, sliced crosswise
2 medium carrots, sliced into matchsticks

GRAVY
1 tablespoon cornstarch
1 cup water, divided
1½ cups chicken broth
¼ cup ketchup
3 tablespoons brown sugar
3 tablespoons white or rice vinegar
2 teaspoons salt
1 teaspoon soy sauce

7.75 ounces long rice (cellophane noodles), softened in hot water 30 minutes
1 medium tomato, wedged

Combine beef with wine and salt; marinate 10 minutes.

Heat 2 tablespoons oil in wok or skillet; Add beef, stir-fry 1 minute; remove and set aside. Heat remaining 1 tablespoon oil; stir-fry celery, pepper, onions, and carrots 1 to 2 minutes.

In a bowl, mix cornstarch with ¼ cup water. Set aside. Mix remaining water and remaining ingredients. Add to vegetables along with drained long rice. Stir to blend ingredients and cook until gravy thickens. Add cooked beef with tomatoes; simmer 3 minutes. Serve with hot steamed rice.

Variations: Substitute pork or chicken for beef.

CHICKEN/TURKEY RICE PORRIDGE

Gai/For Gai Jook

MAKES 6 TO 8SERVINGS

A great recipe for utilizing the bones of roast chicken or turkey. It is truly a comfort food—especially on cold winter nights and is a great way to stretch your food dollar. Depending on your tastes, Jook can be made thick (8 parts water to 1 part rice) or thinner (12 parts water to 1 part rice). This is also called congee by the British in Hong Kong.

Chicken or turkey bones
3 quarts water
1 cup long, medium, or short grain rice, washed and drained
2 pieces dried black mushrooms, softened in hot water, stems discarded and caps slivered
1½ teaspoons salt
½ teaspoon Shaoxing wine or dry sherry
½ chung choy (salted preserved turnip), minced
Minced green onion for garnish
Chinese parsley for garnish

Place bones in large kettle with water to cover; bring to a boil and simmer 45 to 60 minutes or until meat separates from bones.

Remove bones; add rice, mushrooms, salt, wine, and chung choy. Simmer 1 to 2 hours over low heat, adding water as necessary to achieve the consistency you enjoy.

Adjust seasoning and garnish with green onion and Chinese parsley to serve.

Additional condiments to serve with jook include minced chung choy, chopped sweet pickled cucumbers (cha qwa), thousand-year-old eggs (pei dan), salted duck eggs (ham dan), and fresh lettuce. Some people enjoy jook with a dash of toasted sesame oil or hot chili oil.

SINGAPORE NOODLES
Sing Chau Mai Fun

MAKES ABOUT 10 SERVINGS

Our naming of foods is so humorous. We call them French Fries, but the French don't claim them. We call this stir-fried rice noodle dish with curry flavoring Singapore noodles, but those in that country don't know what we are talking about. In any case, this combination has become a standard offering in Hawai'i dim sum restaurants. It is colorful as well as tasty.

8 ounces dried rice noodles (mai fun)
4 tablespoons oil, divided
2 large eggs, beaten
1 cup slivered char siu
¾ cup sliced onions
12 large shrimp, peeled and deveined
1 medium carrot, peeled and sliced into matchsticks
½ red bell pepper, cored and slivered, substitute green bell pepper or other vegetables
½ green bell pepper, cored and slivered
1 teaspoon minced garlic
1½ tablespoons yellow curry powder
½ teaspoon salt
½ teaspoon white pepper
1 tablespoon Shaoxing wine, substitute dry sherry
1 tablespoon soy sauce
1 tablespoon oyster sauce, substitute fish sauce
Jalapeños, dried chili, or fresh chili (optional)
¼ to ½ cup chicken broth
2 teaspoons sesame oil
¾ cup green onions, cut into 1-inch slices
10 ounces bean sprouts
Chinese parsley or slivered green onions for garnish
Other substitutions: snow peas, green beans, mushrooms, roast pork, chicken, lap cheong sausage, bok choy, won bok, head cabbage

The night before, soak the noodles in water and refrigerate overnight. Or soak in hot water for 30 minutes. Drain noodles in a colander and cut them into 6-inch lengths using scissors, so they are easier to eat.

Ingredients are cooked in batches so each one is the right consistency. Heat a wok or cast-iron skillet on medium high heat. Add 1 tablespoon oil and add beaten eggs. When the edges are cooked, flip over and break into smaller pieces. When almost thoroughly cooked, about 3 minutes, remove from wok and set aside.

Add 1 tablespoon oil, on medium-high heat and stir-fry char siu and onions together until onions are translucent, about 3 to 5 minutes. Remove from wok and set aside.

Add 1 tablespoon oil and stir-fry shrimp, carrots, and red and green bell peppers until almost cooked, about 3 minutes. Set aside.

Add last tablespoon oil and put in curry powder, salt, white pepper, Shaoxing wine, soy sauce, oyster sauce with noodles and stir for about 3 minutes. Add chili if using. Gradually add chicken broth and sesame oil and cook until noodles are almost the texture you like. Add in all ingredients you had set aside. When thoroughly cooked, turn off heat and add green onions and bean sprouts. Serve immediately with Chinese parsley as garnish. Serve with a hot sauce (page 170).

FRIED NOODLES WITH THREE MEATS
Sam See Mein

MAKES 6 TO 8 SERVINGS

This noodle dish is favored by many in Hawai'i because it is flavored by the delicious blend of three different items—chicken, pork, and shrimp—and cooked with many vegetables.

- 1/4 cup vegetable oil, divided use
- 1 small onion, thinly sliced
- 1 stalk celery, thinly sliced
- 1/4 cup sliced carrots, cut in matchstick strips
- 1 small green bell pepper, thinly sliced, substitute green beans
- 1/2 cup bamboo shoots, cut into matchstick strips
- 1 cup bean sprouts, rinsed and drained
- 2 teaspoons oyster sauce
- 1/2 teaspoon salt
- Dash of white pepper
- 1/2 cup sliced boneless, skinless chicken breasts or thighs
- 1/4 cup chopped Chinese roast pork (siu jee yuk)
- 1/2 cup raw shrimp, peeled, deveined and chopped
- 1 pound fresh chow mein noodles

GRAVY

- 1½ teaspoons cornstarch
- 1 cup chicken broth
- 1 teaspoon soy sauce
- Dash of salt
- 1½ tablespoons water

Chinese parsley for garnish

Heat 2 tablespoons oil in wok or large skillet. Sauté onion, celery, carrots, green pepper, bamboo shoots, bean sprouts, oyster sauce, salt, and pepper for 2 to 3 minutes over high heat; remove from pan.

Heat remaining 2 tablespoons oil and stir-fry chicken, roast pork, and shrimp 2 to 3 minutes over high heat.

Place noodles in a baking pan and heat in 350°F oven for 15 minutes.

Make the gravy in a separate bowl. Dissolve cornstarch in half of the chicken broth, stir in remaining ingredients including remaining chicken broth and add to chicken mixture; simmer over low heat for 2 minutes. Remove heated noodles from oven and serve on a platter or keep in the baking pan. Mix in cooked vegetables with gravy and meats; pour over noodles.

Garnish with Chinese parsley, if desired. Serve immediately with sauce of your choice (page 170).

STIR-FRIED CHICKEN NOODLES

Gai See Chow Mein

MAKES 4 TO 6 SERVINGS

Thin noodles turn delightfully crispy when fried in oil. Topped with vegetables and slices of chicken, Gai See Chow Mein is an enjoyable meal. You really can add any type of vegetable that you have on hand—bok choy, won bok, asparagus, or green cabbage.

- 1/4 cup vegetable oil, divided
- 1 pound fresh chow mein noodles (Hong Kong-style thin noodles preferred) *
- 1/2 cup sliced raw chicken, breasts or thighs
- 1 small onion, thinly sliced
- 1/4 cup sliced carrots, cut in matchstick strips
- 5 green beans, cut in 1/4-inch slant strips
- 1 cup bean sprouts, rinsed and drained
- 1 1/2 teaspoons oyster sauce
- 1/2 teaspoon salt
- Dash of white pepper

GRAVY

- 1 1/2 teaspoons cornstarch
- 1 cup chicken broth
- 1 teaspoon soy sauce
- Dash of salt
- 1 1/2 tablespoons water

Chinese parsley for garnish, optional

Heat 2 tablespoons oil in wok or large skillet and heat noodles* on both sides over medium-high heat until crisp; remove and set aside on serving platter.

Stir-fry chicken in remaining 2 tablespoons oil. Add onion, carrots, beans, bean sprouts, oyster sauce, salt, and pepper and stir-fry for 1 to 2 minutes over high heat.

In separate bowl make the gravy. Dissolve cornstarch in chicken broth, stir in remaining ingredients and add to chicken mixture; simmer over low heat for 2 minutes. Pour vegetable mixture over crisp noodles. Garnish with Chinese parsley, if desired. Serve with simple hot mustard and soy sauce or another sauce (page 170).

This dish is my grandchildren's most favorite Chinese food. Of course, they have many others they enjoy, but their faces light up when Gai See Chow Mein is brought to the table. There are many versions of this recipe and we'd like to share our family's recipe with you.

—Muriel

* Follow package directions. Some noodles need to be immersed in boiling water for a minute before heating in oil.

A traditional Chinese cleaver can be used to chop vegetables.

BAKED FRIED NOODLES
Gon Lo Mein

MAKES 4 TO 6 SERVINGS

This is one of the most popular noodle dishes in Hawai'i. When you're in a hurry and need a side dish that'll be ready in less than 25 minutes with no fuss or bother, gon lo mein should be your go-to dish. Just toss everything together and pop it into the oven.

- 1 pound fresh thin chow mein or thick lo mein noodles
- 10 ounces bean sprouts, rinsed and drained
- ½ cup diced celery, cut thinly diagonally
- ½ cup 1-inch length green onions
- 1 cup slivered char siu
- 1 tablespoon toasted sesame seeds
- ¾ cup raw, cleaned shrimp (optional)

SEASONING

- 2 tablespoons oyster sauce
- ¼ cup chicken broth
- 2 tablespoon vegetable oil
- 1 tablespoon sesame oil
- 1 teaspoon salt

GARNISH

- 2 tablespoons toasted sesame seeds
- ¼ cup Chinese parsley
- ¼ cup slivered char siu

In a 9 × 13-inch baking pan, mix together noodles, bean sprouts, celery, green onion, char siu, sesame seeds, and shrimp, if using. Sprinkle with seasonings toss to mix well. Seal with foil. Bake at 350°F for 15 to 20 minutes or until heated through. Check that noodles have been cooked. Add garnishes and serve hot.

In this cookbook, we refer to Chinese parsley. In other parts of the country, it is referred to as cilantro or fresh coriander.

STIR-FRIED FLAT NOODLES WITH PORK
Chow Fun

MAKES 4 TO 6 SERVINGS

The silky texture of steamed noodles (look fun or hor fun) is stir-fried (chow) to give this dish its name. Any combination of toppings can be added, but there is always a variety of colorful vegetables to provide the welcome crunch. The contrast of the soft noodles with succulent pork and crisp vegetables makes this noodle dish a favorite.

½ pound pork, cut into strips*
½-inch piece fresh ginger, minced
½ teaspoon salt
2 teaspoons soy sauce
1 teaspoon sugar
1 tablespoon vegetable oil
½ pound green beans, finely sliced, diagonally
1 small carrot, finely sliced
10 ounces bean sprouts
1 celery stalk, sliced thinly, diagonally
2 stalks green onion, cut in 1-inch lengths

SEASONINGS
¼ cup chicken broth
2 teaspoons salt
¼ teaspoon pepper
½ teaspoon oyster sauce
½ teaspoon Shaoxing wine or dry sherry

2 rolls fresh look fun noodles, cut in ¼-inch strips (bought or recipe for Cheung Fun on page 8)

Chinese parsley for garnish

This used to be a favorite after-school snack for me as a youngster. It can be eaten hot or cold.
—Muriel

Combine pork strips with ginger, salt, soy sauce, and sugar; stir to mix well and let stand 15 minutes.

Stir-fry pork in hot oil in large skillet or wok on high heat until brown. Add vegetables and seasonings; stir-fry additional minute. Add noodles; cover until noodles are heated through. Stir quickly to mix ingredients. Garnish with Chinese parsley to serve.

Variations: Chicken or beef may be substituted for pork.

Tip: Dried packaged chow fun noodles may be substituted for fresh noodles. Cook noodles as directed on package. Fresh noodles often get mushy if stirred too much.

*Use pork tenderloin, butt, or shoulder cuts.

Sauces

In Hawai'i, Chinese restaurants that serve dim sum may have tables set with a few dishes of condiments and sauces including hot mustard, chili oil or chili paste, red vinegar, and soy sauce. However, outside of Hawai'i, we have noticed that the table may only be set with condiments that are appropriate for the dishes ordered. Also, in some areas, the condiment tray may also include salt and pepper mixture, sweet and sour sauce, soy sauce mixed with vinegar, ginger, scallions, or sugar. With certain dishes, diners expect specific sauces. For example, with Steamed Rolls filled with shrimp, scallops, or green onions (page 8) sweet soy sauce is expected. Some cannot eat Singapore Noodles (page 160) without red vinegar or hot mustard.

With just the addition of a dipping sauce, a dish can become more interesting with a texture (Chinese Parsley Sauce with Cucumbers) or spicy from chili peppers (Spicy Soy Sauce Vinegar Sauce). Your friends will appreciate your level of care for them by offering several dipping sauces. Let them select their own level of spice.

HOT MUSTARD

MAKES ABOUT 1/3 CUP

You can buy this in a jar, but it is easy to make in small quantities to enjoy at full potency. Served as a dip in small dishes. It is particularly good with deep-fried foods—egg rolls, wontons, and batter-coated shrimp and chicken—and is often paired with ketchup.

1/4 cup hot dry mustard powder
1/4 cup cold water
1/8 teaspoon vegetable oil

Place mustard in a bowl. Gradually stir in cold water until smooth. Stir in oil. Cover and let stand for 1 hour for the flavor to mellow.

Use immediately, or transfer to a small jar, cover, and refrigerate up to a month.

Commonly served with a container of soy sauce so diners can mix the mustard-soy sauce to their preferred proportions.

CHILI OIL

MAKES 1/2 CUP

For sparkling hot flavor, add a few drops of this oil while cooking stir-fried dishes, or pass at the table in a small cruet. It is good with noodles or steamed dim sum, especially when used with vinegar and soy sauce.

1/3 cup vegetable oil
3 tablespoons sesame oil
6 small, dry, hot chili peppers or 2 tablespoons crushed red pepper

In a small pan, heat oils over medium heat. When oil is hot but not smoking, add chili peppers and stir for 1 minute. Remove from heat and cool.

Strain and discard peppers. Store refrigerated in a covered jar for up to a year.

HOT PEPPER & BLACK BEAN SAUCE

MAKES ABOUT 1/2 CUP

This is a great sauce for stir-fried and steamed dishes; use sparingly as it packs a punch.

- **1/3 cup peanut, vegetable, or canola oil**
- **3 tablespoons crushed red pepper**
- **1½ tablespoons dow see (fermented black beans), rinsed and drained**
- **1 tablespoon minced garlic**
- **2 teaspoons Shaoxing wine, substitute dry sherry**
- **2 teaspoons toasted sesame oil**
- **½ teaspoon salt**

Combine all ingredients in a heat-proof jar or bowl; cover securely with foil and set on rack over simmering water. Cover and steam 45 minutes.

Cool completely; cover and refrigerate. Serve at room temperature. Keep refrigerated in a container for up to 1 month.

SPICY SOY DIPPING SAUCE

MAKES ABOUT 1 CUP

Delicious as a dipping sauce for potstickers and other dumplings.

- **1/3 cup soy sauce**
- **1/3 cup rice vinegar**
- **1/3 cup minced green onion**
- **1 tablespoon toasted sesame oil**
- **1 tablespoon sambal oelek (Indonesian chili sauce)**

Combine all ingredients; mix well. Will keep refrigerated in an airtight container for a few days. Best if served fresh.

SPICY SOY VINEGAR SAUCE

MAKES ABOUT ½ CUP

This popular sauce is very similar to Japanese ponzu sauce—delicious with potstickers! This has a punch from the chili sauce.

¼ cup soy sauce
2 tablespoons rice vinegar
1 tablespoon sugar
1 tablespoon water
1 tablespoon sambal oelek (Indonesian chili sauce)
1 teaspoon minced green onion

Combine all ingredients except green onion in small saucepan; heat over low heat until sugar dissolves.

Sprinkle green onions before serving. Best used fresh since green onions are included. Keep refrigerated for a few days.

SWEET SOY SAUCE

MAKES ABOUT ½ CUP

Pour this sauce over steamed flour rolls (Cheung Fun) just as it is being served. Recipe for those delicate rolls on page 8.

⅓ cup water
¼ cup soy sauce
2 tablespoons sugar
2 teaspoons toasted sesame oil
1 tablespoon thinly sliced green onion

Combine all ingredients except green onion in small saucepan; heat over low heat until sugar dissolves.

Sprinkle green onions over before serving. Keep refrigerated for up to one week.

SWEET-AND-SOUR SAUCE

MAKES ABOUT 2 CUPS

Use over Gau Gee (page 24), other fried dumplings, seafood, meats, and also as a dip.

1½ cups pineapple juice, canned or fresh
2 tablespoons ketchup
2 teaspoons tomato paste
2½ tablespoons brown sugar
3 tablespoons apple cider vinegar

Combine all ingredients in a saucepan and bring to a boil over medium heat.

Reduce heat and simmer 5 to 8 minutes, stirring frequently, until sugar dissolves. Alternatively, mix 1 teaspoon cornstarch with 1 tablespoon cold water until dissolved. Add into mixture and cook over medium heat until thickened, about 3 minutes. Cool before serving.

SWEET CHILI SAUCE

MAKES ABOUT ½ CUP

A spicy sauce with a sweet edge that enhances noodle dishes and dumplings.

½ cup mirin (Japanese sweet rice wine)
1 tablespoon minced green onion
2 teaspoons sambal oelek (Indonesian chili sauce)
1 teaspoon sugar

Combine all ingredients and mix well. Keep in refrigerator for up to one week.

SWEET CHILI AIOLI

MAKES ABOUT 1/2 CUP

1/2 cup mayonnaise

3 tablespoons Sweet Chili Sauce (page 174)

Stir ingredients together to create an aioli, which basically means mayonnaise is involved; serve with fried dishes. Store refrigerated for up to a week.

SALT AND PEPPER WITH CHINESE FIVE SPICE POWDER MIXTURE

MAKES ABOUT 2 1/2 TABLESPOONS

1 1/2 tablespoons salt
2 teaspoons ground white pepper
1/4 teaspoon Chinese Five Spice powder

Combine ingredients in a blender. Blend to a fine texture. Heat mixture in a nonstick skillet without oil for 25 seconds. Remove from heat and cool. Use for Salt and Pepper Fried Shrimp (page 113) or serve as a condiment when serving Roast Duck (page 142) or Peking Duck (page 140). Will keep in an airtight container, unrefrigerated for up to 1 month.

SWEET AND HOT CHINESE PARSLEY SAUCE

MAKES ABOUT 1½ CUPS

A nice dipping sauce for fried dumplings and spring rolls.

- ¾ cup white vinegar
- ¼ cup sugar
- ¼ cup water
- 1 small Hawaiian chili pepper, seeded and minced
- ¼ cup minced green onion
- 2 tablespoons minced Chinese parsley
- ½ cup seeded and chopped cucumber

Combine vinegar, sugar, and water in small saucepan. Cook over low heat, stirring frequently, until sugar dissolves.

Turn off heat; stir in remaining ingredients.

Best served fresh while cucumbers are crunchy.

GINGER SOY DIPPING SAUCE

MAKES ABOUT ¾ CUP

A very familiar flavor that is often used as a dipping sauce for dumplings.

- ¼ cup soy sauce
- ¼ cup Chinese red vinegar, substitute cider or rice vinegar
- ¼ cup minced green onion
- 1 teaspoon minced fresh ginger
- 1 teaspoon red pepper flakes
- 1 teaspoon sugar

Combine all ingredients; mix well. Store in a container in the refrigerator for up to 1 month.

GLOSSARY
OF CHINESE INGREDIENTS

Bao: Chinese term for bun or bread.

Bean curd (Dow fu/ Dou fu): Tofu made from soybeans.

Bean cake, fermented (Fu yu or **dow fu mui):** White glossy, shiny, soft fermented soybean cake used as condiment or flavoring agent.

Bean curd cake (Nam yu): Red, preserved/fermented soybean curd used as seasoning.

Bean sauce (Min see): Also called brown or yellow bean sauce or soybean condiment. It is made from soybeans, sugar, salt, sesame oil, and flour.

Bean threads (cellophane or **vermicelli bean threads):** Made from mung beans.

Bitter melon (Fu gwa): Balsam pear; vegetable with bitter flavor.

Black beans (Dow see): Tiny salted fermented soybeans with a strong flavor.

Bok choy: A leafy vegetable with white stalks and dark-green leaves.

Chinese slab sugar (Wong tong): Brown sugar made into flat bars.

Chili oil (Lot yau): A spicy condiment made from dried chilies, oil, and sometimes garlic, sesame seeds and/or fermented black beans.

Chili paste with garlic (Lot jiu jeung yau): Hot chili paste in a jar.

Chinese broccoli (Gai lan): Variety of broccoli with white flowers.

Chinese cabbage (Won bok): A mild-flavored cabbage. Also known as napa cabbage.

Chinese eggplant (Ngai gwa): Vegetable with smooth, shiny surface.

Chinese Five Spice powder/seasoning (En heong fun): Usually a blend of Chinese star anise, cloves, cinnamon, fennel, and peppercorns. It is light brown colored and used in numerous Chinese dishes.

Chinese parsley/Cilantro (Yuen sai): Highly aromatic bright green herb. Also known as cilantro or coriander.

Chinese peas: Snow peas.

Chinese sausage (Lap cheong): A sweet, thin Chinese sausage.

Choy sum: Bright leafy green vegetable with yellow flowers and tender stalks.

Chow mein noodles: Chinese soft-fried wheat or egg noodles.

Chung choy: Chinese preserved salted turnip.

Cilantro: See *Chinese parsley.*

Cloud ear fungus (Wan yee or **mok ngee):** A crunchy textured fungus when soaked in water. Pepeiao in Hawaiian a.k.a. tree fungus.

Daikon: See *Turnip, Chinese* (Lo bak)

Dow fu: Tofu; bean cake.

Dried bean curd (Fu jook pei): Dried soybean milk residue in sheets or sticks.

Dried scallops (gon bui): Scallops dried to amber discs; need to be soaked or steamed before using.

Egg roll skins/wrappers (Chun guen pi or **pei):** Flour pastry dough used for various spring rolls; available at most markets in refrigerator or freezer sections.

Fishcake: Raw paste made from the flesh of bonefish such as ʻōʻio or awaawa.

Fish sauce: Strong-flavored sauce made with fish extract, water, and salt.

Foo yu sauce: A sauce made of cubes of pressed bean curd fermented in wine used in cooking.

Ginkgo nuts: Seeds of the ginkgo tree, a common shade tree in China.

Glutinous rice flour (No mai): Flour milled from glutinous rice a.k.a. mochiko or sweet rice flour.

Hoisin sauce (Hoisin cheung): A deep brownish-red sauce made from soybeans, sugar, chili, garlic, Chinese Five Spice powder, and vinegar.

Jicama (Sah gut): A bulbous root, sweet and crisp; use as substitute for water chestnuts.

Jujubes (Hung jo): Olive-sized red fruit also called red dates; need to be soaked before using to add sweetness.

Lichee/Lychee: A round, sweet juicy white fruit covered with a rough, red skin.

Lily bud (Gum choy): 2-inch long flower of the day lily plant; dried.

Longan: Same family as lychee; round with smooth, buff-colored skin; translucent round fruit and sweet when fresh.

Long rice (Fun see): Mung bean flour aka bean threads, Chinese Vermicelli, transparent noodle.

Look fun: Steamed Chinese rice noodles made in wide sheets a.k.a. horfun.

Lotus leaves: Leaves of lotus plant; sold dried and used as food wrapper.

Lotus root (Lin see): A gourd-shaped root of lotus.

Mung bean noodles: Bean thread, glass, long rice, or cellophane noodles.

Mushrooms, Chinese black (Doong goo): Dried, black, gray, or speckled black and gray. Also called shiitake mushrooms.

Mustard greens/ cabbage (Gai choy): A bitter, green vegetable with a thick stem and wide, curved leaves.

Oyster sauce (Hau yau): A thick, rich, brown sauce made from dried oysters, salt, and water. Used as a condiment or seasoning.

Pickled mustard greens (Tsin choy): Sweet pickled gai choy.

Plum sauce (Sheung moy cheung): A thick, amber sauce made from plums with a pungent, spicy flavor. This chutney-like sauce is often used as a condiment.

Potsticker wrappers: Round wheat flour wrappers that are slightly thicker than wonton wrappers.

Red bean paste (Dow sa): Cooked and sweetened deep-red adzuki or kidney beans; generally used in sweets or sweet soups; in paste form which is generally used as filling for pastries.

Red bean curd (Nam yu): A sauce made from soybeans, glutinous red rice, salt, and alcohol.

Red dates (Hung jo): These dried dates are also known as jujubes.

Rice noodles (Fun): A soft, white, flat noodle made from flour and often used like crepes in dim sum items.

Rice paper wrappers: Made from rice flour, water, and salt. These wrappers are brittle and paper thin; dipped in water before used and may be eaten raw or fried.

Rice powder: Ground powder of short-grain rice. Not to be confused with sweet rice flour (no mai fan).

Rice sticks (Mai fun): Rice stick noodles.

Rice vinegar: Vinegar made from fermented rice.

Rice wine (No mai chang): Wine made from rice.

Rock sugar (Bing tong): Similar to rock candy, crystallized sugar; used as a sweetener.

Salt & pepper mixture: (see page 175)

Salted preserved turnips (Chung choy): Used as seasoning ingredient or used as substitute for salt in meat dishes or soups.

Sambal oelek: Spicy Indonesian paste made of ground chili peppers combined with salt, vinegar, and sometimes garlic and tamarind.

Sesame oil (Ma yau): A seasoning oil with a nut-like flavor.

Shrimp paste (Harm Ha): Thick, fishy, salty paste made from fermented shrimp used for flavoring.

Shrimp, dried (Ha mai): Small dried shrimp that are used to impart a delicate flavor to foods.

Snow pea shoots (Dau miu): Tender vines of snow pea.

Soybean: Oval, pale green beans; called edamame in Japanese.

Soy sauce (See yau): A brown seasoning sauce made from fermented soybean extract combined with salt, wheat, and yeast; available as dark, heavy, and light. There are no standards for soy sauce taste.

Spring roll wrappers: Thin sheets of rice flour dough; also called spring roll skins.

Star anise (Bat gok/Juk soon): A small cluster of dark-brown, dry seeds shaped like an eight-pointed flower.

Sweet bean paste: A puréed red, black, or yellow bean paste used as a filling in many Chinese pastries.

Sichuan peppercorns: Also called anise pepper and wild pepper; tangy brown pepper corns or small seeds; mildly hot with pleasing pungent aroma.

Tangerine peel, dried (Chun pei or **Gwo pei):** Skin of tangerine used for flavoring.

Tapioca starch or **powder (Ling fun, tapioca powder):** Starch from the cassava root. Basic ingredient in dumpling dough.

Taro (Woo tau): The starchy root of a tropical plant. Chinese variety is grown on dry land.

Thai sweet chili sauce: Sriracha sauce; mild, sweet chili sauce used as a flavoring and as a dipping sauce.

Tiger lily buds (Gum choy): Light flower buds that have been dried, a.k.a. "golden needles."

Tofu (Doufu/dow fu): White protein rich soybean cake.

Tofu skin (Foo juk or **Foo pei):** The dried layer of skin off the top of boiling soy milk; sold as dried skins or as sticks. Also found vacuum packed fresh.

Turnip, Chinese (Lo bak): White vegetable that looks like an overgrown horseradish. Similar to daikon.

Water chestnuts (Ma tai): A bulb-like vegetable grown in water, savored for its crunch.

Watercress: Member of the mustard family; its small dark green leaves are slightly bitter.

Wheat starch (Dung mein fun): Finely ground substance of what remains of wheat flour when the wheat's protein has been removed to make gluten. Used in making certain types of wrappers in dim sum pastries.

Winter melon (Doong gwa): Very large dark green gourd or squash that looks like watermelon.

Won bok: Chinese or celery cabbage; napa cabbage. The large, light green leaves with white stems are crisp and mild flavored.

Wood or **cloud ears (Wan yee, Chin ngee** or **Mok ngee):** Large, dried, brownish-black fungus; must be soaked in warm water before using. Called pepeiao in Hawaiian.

Wun tun/Wonton: Chinese dumplings usually filled with meat.

Wun tun/Wonton wrappers (Wun tun pi or **pei):** Thin squares of wheat or egg-based dough used to wrap a variety of fillings.

INDEX

C

D

E

F

N

O

P

R

S

T

W

Y

Muriel Miura may be most recognized for her 1970s nationally televised cooking shows, *Cook Japanese Hawaiian Style* and *The New World of Cooking with Muriel*. (She was the first local chef to have her own TV program and the first woman in Hawai'i to have a TV show.) While comfortable with all types of cuisine, Muriel's specialty was Japanese cooking where she added a personal touch of Hawai'i to her dishes.

Muriel was a prolific author, writing more than twenty-five cookbooks including *Cookies from Hawai'i's Kitchen, Hawai'i Cooks with Spam, Hawai'i Cooks and Saves, Celebrating in Hawai'i, What Hawai'i Likes to Eat*, and *A Japanese Kitchen*. She also served as co-editor of the "Hawai'i Cooks" series that featuring *A Korean Kitchen, A Portuguese Kitchen, An Okinawan Kitchen, A Chinese Kitchen*, and *A Filipino Kitchen*. Her latest cookbook *Home Cooking, Hawai'i-Style* was released in fall of 2021.

Throughout her culinary career, she judged food contests, taught community cooking classes and high school home economics, wrote articles about cuisine and food, and traveled to the New York World's Fair as a featured presenter where she won a prestigious award for outstanding demonstration. Muriel also guest-starred on the popular *Hari's Kitchen TV* cooking show.

Muriel graduated from the University of Hawai'i's Home Economics program and earned graduate degrees in Home Economics Education from the University of Hawai'i at Mānoa and Columbia University in New York City.

She was the director of Home Economics at The Gas Company until 1993. Following her retirement, besides writing cookbooks, she was involved with a number of community service projects and served on the Board of Directors and Board of Trustees of the Mō'ili'ili Community Center.

OTHER BOOKS BY MURIEL MIURA

AS AUTHOR

Cook Japanese Hawaiian Style (Listed as Best-Seller), 1974

Hawaiian Pūpū Party Planner, 1974 • *Hawaiian Potpourri*, 1975

Maxi Meals for Mini Money, 1975 • *Cook Japanese Hawaiian Style Volume II*, 1976

New World of Cooking with Muriel, 1979 • *Cooking with Hari and Muriel*, 1994

From Hawai'i's Kitchen: Homemade Gifts of Sweets & Treats, 2005*

Holiday Gift Giving Recipes, 2005*

Little Hawaiian Holiday Gift-Giving Recipes, 2005* • *Hawai'i's Party Food*, 2007*

Japanese Cooking Hawai'i Style, 2006* • *Little Hawaiian Party Food Cookbook*, 2007*

Little Hawaiian Cookbooks: Tastes & Flavors of Pineapple, 2007*

What Hawai'i Likes to Eat, 2007* • *Hawai'i Cooks with Spam®*, 2008*

Hawai'i Cooks & Saves, 2008* • *What Hawai'i Likes to Eat, Hana Hou*, 2009*

Little Hawaiian Condiments Cookbook, 2011*

Little Hawaiian Japanese Cooking Hawai'i Style, 2011*

Celebrating in Hawai'i: Favorite Recipes for Holidays and Special Occasions, 2016*

Favorite Recipes from the What Hawai'i Likes to Eat Series, 2016*

Hawai'i Cooks: A Japanese Kitchen, 2017*

Home Cooking, Hawai'i-Style, 2021*

AS EDITOR/CHAIR

Heritage of Hawai'i: Cookbook vol. I (Gasco), 1965

Heritage of Hawai'i: Cookbook vol. II (Gasco), 1970

The Legacy of the Japanese in Hawai'i: Cuisine (JCCH), 1989

Tastes & Tales of Mōili'ili (Mōili'ili Community Center), 1997*

A Tradition of Aloha Cookbook (Japanese Women's Society), 1998

Flavors of Aloha (Japanese Women's Society), 2001

Hawai'i Cooks: A Korean Kitchen, 2013* • *Hawai'i Cooks: An Okinawan Kitchen*, 2014*

Hawai'i Cooks: A Portuguese Kitchen, 2014* • *Hawai'i Cooks: A Chinese Kitchen*, 2015*

Hawai'i Cooks: A Filipino Kitchen, 2016* • *A Taste of Aloha Favorites*, 2019*

*Published by Mutual Publishing

Lynette Lo Tom relaxes by cooking and considers it her art. She is the author of *A Chinese Kitchen*, part of the "Hawai'i Cooks" series of cookbooks that highlights the ethnic diversity that is our state. She also authored *Back in the Day* cookbook, which won the 2019 Ka Palapala Po'okela Award of Excellence from the Hawai'i Book Publishers Association.

Lynette is a freelance food writer and regular contributor to several publications. Her columns in the *Honolulu Star-Advertiser* are "Back in the Day" and "Easy-Kine Cooking."

She was born and raised in Honolulu. Lynette holds a journalism degree from the University of Colorado at Boulder and an MBA degree from the University of California at Berkeley.

Before she started writing about food and cooking through Bright Light Cookery, she was a journalist, then a marketing and public relations consultant with her own company named Bright Light Marketing. Contact her at lynette@brightlightcookery.com.

OTHER BOOKS BY LYNETTE LO TOM

Hawai'i Cooks: A Chinese Kitchen, 2015*
Back in the Day, 2018*

*Published by Mutual Publishing